Choral Conducting

CHORAL CONDUCTING

Abraham Kaplan
University of Washington

W·W·NORTON & COMPANY
New York and London

Copyright © 1985 by W. W. Norton & Company, Inc.

All rights reserved.

Printed in the United States of America.

This book is composed in Palatino. Composition by Vail-Ballou. Manufacturing by
The Maple-Vail Book Group.
Book design by Win Potter

First Edition

Library of Congress Cataloging in Publication Data

Kaplan, Abraham.
  Choral Conducting.

  1. Conducting, Choral.   I. Title.
MT85.K3278   1985   784.9'63   84-25559

ISBN 0-393-97705-6

W. W. Norton & Company, Inc., 500 Fifth Avenue, New York, N.Y. 10110
W. W. Norton & Company Ltd., 10 Coptic Street, London WC1A 1PU

0

To
MICHAEL, DAFNA, DAVID and DAVIDA
With Love

Contents

Preface

During my thirty-year career as a choral conductor, orchestral conductor, and teacher of choral conducting, I have often felt the need for a textbook that streamlines and organizes the teaching of a subject that defies organization. I searched for a book that would include not only explanations but also simply arranged exercises for systematic training in basic conducting skills. In the incredibly vast collection of books on both choral and orchestral conducting, I did not find one that satisfactorily accomplishes this task, and so, for the past thirty years, I have found myself inadvertently writing this book.

The purpose of this book is to provide a much needed text that can be used daily by choral conducting teachers and students on the university level. My intent is that this manual will allow the instructor to cover every aspect of conducting and rehearsal techniques.

The book consists of exercises in conducting with diagrams and musical examples, allowing each student the opportunity actually to conduct in the classroom.

Also included are essays on subjects with which a choral conductor must become familiar if he or she is to develop a sound rehearsal technique.

At the end of many of the exercises I have suggested some choral selections under "Suggested Repertoire." These selections give the conductor the chance to practice the technical problems discussed in the preceding exercises within a musical context.*

Following is a sample of how I structure a one-hour session using the book:

1. The class practices conducting the exercises found in Chapter Four from the sections "Fermata" and "Beats That May Be Omitted." (10 minutes)
2. Two or three students take turns rehearsing and conducting short choral pieces. These can be assigned from the Suggested Repertoire. (25 minutes)

*The Appendix provides a more extensive annotated Suggested Repertoire.

3. Class discussion of Chapter Four, "Rehearsing Slow Music." (15 minutes)

It is my fervent hope that this book will clarify and facilitate the teaching of choral conducting on both the beginning and advanced levels.

ACKNOWLEDGMENTS

I would like to express my gratitude:

To Bob Markel, a dear friend and colleague who first suggested the writing of this book twenty years ago and who is the man most responsible for its publication;

To Claire Brook, Music Editor of W. W. Norton, whose professional advice as to the format of this book has been invaluable;

To Mrs. Angela DeSimone, who, while typing this manuscript, manifested a relentless drive for perfection;

To Doctor Eugen Grabscheid, whose advice concerning voice and vocal production was extremely helpful;

To Madeleine Marshal, whose course on English Diction was the most beneficial single course in my education as a musician and choral conductor;

And last, but not least to my students, whose fertile talents and probing questions compelled me to think clearly.

Introduction

What is Choral Conducting?

In order to answer this question and understand clearly what one is trying to accomplish when practicing the art of choral conducting, it is imperative to consider the three most important components which make choral conducting what it is: 1) the music, 2) the chorus, and 3) the conducting.

The Music

Of all the answers given to the question "what is music?", the one that seems to me to be the most illuminating is "Music is a language!" Like other languages devised by the human race, it is a means of communication; but unlike most other languages which utilize words and sentences, music (without text) cannot communicate messages such as "Please give me a glass of water," "I love you," or even "There is a storm outside." Music's realm of communication is much more abstract and touches us in ways that cannot be described adequately by words. We could say that music starts where words end.

The Chorus

The chorus (like the orchestra) is one of the most exciting musical instruments devised by Western civilization.

Conducting

Conducting is the incredible art of "playing" that instrument. Choral conducting, therefore, must be considered as conducting into which is incorporated a thorough knowledge of the instrument (the chorus), its limitations, as well as its unending potential.

What Do You Do as a Conductor?

Your first and most obvious task is to beat time properly and keep your ensemble together rhythmically. Your second and more difficult task is to rehearse the ensemble with the objective of communicating the musical images of your inner ear. To accomplish both you must study the music until it becomes part of you.

This book is designed to train you to accomplish both tasks with proficiency and imagination.

The Emergence of Conducting as a Profession

The first conductors were members of the performing groups they conducted. In addition to their singing or playing duties, they had the responsibility of indicating the start and end of the performance.

As ensembles grew in size, it eventually became necessary to have someone keep the players rhythmically together during the performance. At this stage, the conductor stood in front of his ensemble facing the audience and beating time with a long stick.

Subsequently, conductors (except those who led marching bands) turned around to face the ensemble, shortened the stick, and before anybody understood what was happening, became the "stars" of the musical performance. This ascent to musical stardom was not universally greeted with cheers. As a matter of fact, the only ones who cheered conductors without hesitation (sensing that the great ones were doing something special) were the audiences.

Many musicians playing in orchestras thought—and they were probably right—that conductors were getting too much credit for the good qualities of performances and were rarely blamed for the mishaps. Many argued that conductors were absolutely unnecessary and should be completely eliminated from the musical scene.

Two notable attempts by major symphony orchestras to play regularly without a conductor have recently been made on two sides of the globe.

The first took place in Russia shortly after the Bolshevik revolution. Those in charge of the Moscow Philharmonic decided, for ideological reasons, to have the orchestra play without a conductor.

Approximately fifty years later in New York City, after the dissolution of the NBC Symphony that followed the retirement of Arturo Toscanini, members of the orchestra organized themselves as the Symphony of the Air and also decided to play their concerts without a conductor. Both the Moscow Philharmonic and the Symphony of the Air experiments lasted only a few months before those orchestras went back to the conventional way of playing under the direction of conductors.

The question is: Why? Why can't a competent ensemble, made up of first-rate musicians, play without a conductor? As we have seen, conductors came into being for the purpose of keeping large groups of instrumentalists or singers rhythmically together. Therefore, *unifying the performance rhythmically* was—and still is—the most fundamental role of a conductor.

Since, however, musical rhythms are neither metronomic nor mechanical, the conductor, in controlling the rhythms of musical phrases, controlled their shape as well and affected the beauty of the music.

Conductors started experimenting with slight fluctuations of the tempo and their effect on musical phrases. As imaginative conducting slowly emerged, audiences began to realize that some of those people standing in front of the ensemble seemed to "beat time" in a way that made the music more beautiful than that produced by other "time beaters." Knowing that a conductor would study the complete musical score and could alert the musicians to its special requirements, composers could now require unusual balances between the instruments.

Whereas composers up to Mozart's time had had to write music in which the musical instruments or groups thereof would practically balance themselves, now composers could ask for special effects that the conductor would be responsible for realizing. Thus developed the second important role of the conductor: *maintenance of the proper balance among the different instruments of the orchestra.*

As we can now see, the conductor's role requires a consummate musician with a keen ear as well as great imagination, leadership, and psychological insight. The professional who takes charge of many other persons for the purpose of accomplishing a common goal should have—in addition to all the professional qualifications—the gift of leadership as well.

From my long experience in preparing the Camerata Singers for performances and recordings with the New York Philharmonic under the direction of most of today's greatest conductors, it has become clear that, despite these conductors' incredible variety of talents, temperaments, and personalities, one common denominator prevails: those who earned the respect of the orchestra, and were therefore cheerfully followed, were the ones who were the most thoroughly professional—i.e., those who knew what they wanted and knew how to get it.

And so, to summarize, the conductor is a person who *plays* the most exciting musical instruments devised by Western civilization: the chorus, the orchestra, and the combination of these two. This task is best accomplished by learning the musical score to the point of identifying yourself with it completely and then by transmitting your knowledge and conception of the work to your fellow musicians: first, through your rehearsal technique and finally, at the concert, with the communicative power of your conducting technique.

CHORAL CONDUCTING

Chapter One

CONDUCTING PATTERNS

Baton or No Baton

Observing the work of some of the best conductors of our time leads one to the conclusion that a conductor can achieve great musical results conducting with or without a baton. However, a second look will show that when these great conductors do use a baton, it is invariably an extension of the arm and wrist motion.

The advantages of using a baton are obvious in the following instances:

1. when conducting a very large ensemble;
2. when conducting opera from the pit;
3. When a very crisp and fast beat is desired (mostly in instrumental music).

In the first two instances the presence of the baton helps the performers see the beat. In the third, the small crisp movement of the wrist is thus enlarged and becomes clearly visible to the singers and players.

Whenever a baton is used, special care must be taken that the conductor's elbow never moves in opposition to the baton. Many a conductor has been driven mad by the fact that one section of the orchestra is playing half a beat apart from the rest of the orchestra; but from where they were sitting the conductor's elbow (moving in contrary motion) attracted more attention than the baton.

Left-Handed Conductors

In the 1950s a good friend and colleague, who is left-handed, told me of his experience at Pierre Monteux's master class in conducting. When my friend's turn came, he picked up his baton and waited for the Maestro's

OK to start. Instead, the old man slowly walked toward the podium, took the baton from my friend's left hand and placed it in his right. He did all of this without saying a word. Since that moment my friend has conducted with his right hand.

This story is typical of the traditional attitude concerning the hand that should be used to beat time. However, there is no justification for it, and as we no longer require our children to write with their right hands, there is no reason to insist that left-handed conductors beat time with their right hands.

The conducting diagrams in this book are drawn for the right hand. If you are left-handed you can use the same diagrams as they would be reflected in a mirror. Here is a conducting pattern diagram for the right hand and its equivalent for the left hand:

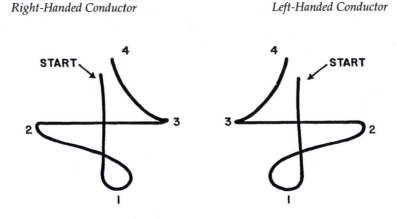

Right-Handed Conductor   *Left-Handed Conductor*

Use either your right or left hand to beat time, but *don't use both.* If you are left-handed apply all that is said in this book about the right hand to your left and vice versa.

Conducting Patterns

The internationally accepted conducting patterns are designed to enable you, through simply shaped motions, to communicate your instructions as to when any given note should be sung or played in relation to your beat.

The Pattern of $\frac{4}{4}$

In a composition written in the meter $\frac{4}{4}$, the conductor will beat the following pattern:

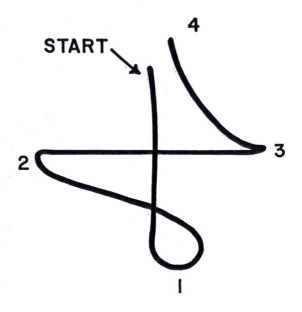

This means that when the conductor's hand is at beat 1 of the diagram above, all singers and players must be singing and playing the notes that appear on the first beat of the first measure of the music as illustrated below.

THOMAS TALLIS, *If Ye Love Me*

When you reach beat 2 of the pattern, the players and singers will be on beat 2 of the music, and so on for the third and fourth beats. In subsequent measures, the same procedure is repeated.

The Preparatory Beat

Before a note is to be sung or played, you beat a *preparatory beat*, which comes in advance of the first beat of the music and therefore represents the beat *preceding* the conducting pattern. For example, if the music starts on beat 1 (as in the excerpt above), the preparatory beat should come on the fourth beat of an *imaginary* preceding measure, as in the diagram on p. 5.

The preparatory beat also serves as a cue for the singers to *breathe*.

EXERCISE 1

The Pattern of $\frac{4}{4}$, including Preparatory Beat

The class stands in a circle; each member takes a turn conducting the $\frac{4}{4}$ pattern with a preparatory beat (see diagram on p. 5, while the other class members try to "predict" when beat 1 will occur by speaking the sound "da," as in Example 1, at the appropriate moment.

EXAMPLE 1

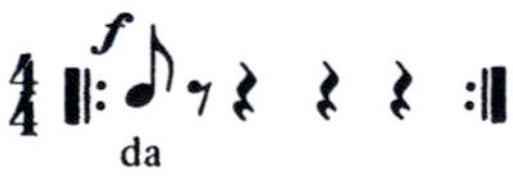

A good preparatory beat will result in unity of class ensemble. An insufficient preparatory beat will result in scattered entrances. A good preparatory beat is a *predictable* beat. Once started, it should be carried through without hesitation.

---

4   *Conducting Patterns*

EXERCISE 2

The Pattern of $\frac{4}{4}$, including Preparatory Beat

A. All class members practice conducting the pattern of $\frac{4}{4}$ starting on a preparatory beat:

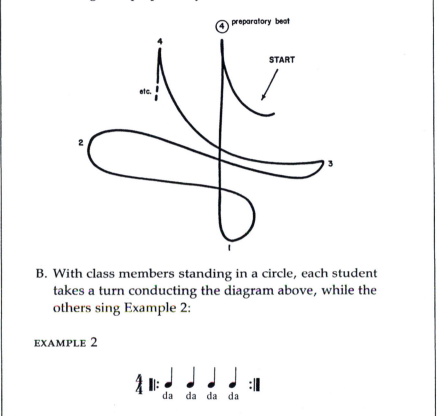

B. With class members standing in a circle, each student takes a turn conducting the diagram above, while the others sing Example 2:

EXAMPLE 2

Each conductor can evaluate the results of this exercise. If the first "da's" were together, then the preparatory beat must have been good and predictable. If all the beats of the entire measure were together, then the entire pattern was good and predictable.

From this exercise, we can conclude that each beat is, in a sense, a preparatory beat for the following one. Just as your preparatory beat (beat 4) affects what happens on the first beat of the music, the way you conduct the first beat of the pattern will affect the response on the second beat of the music, and so on.

In other words, *you must communicate your intentions concerning the music being performed one beat ahead of the ensemble.* A vigorous preparatory beat will elicit a vigorous sound on the first beat of the music, while a gentle, peaceful one will result in a corresponding sound.

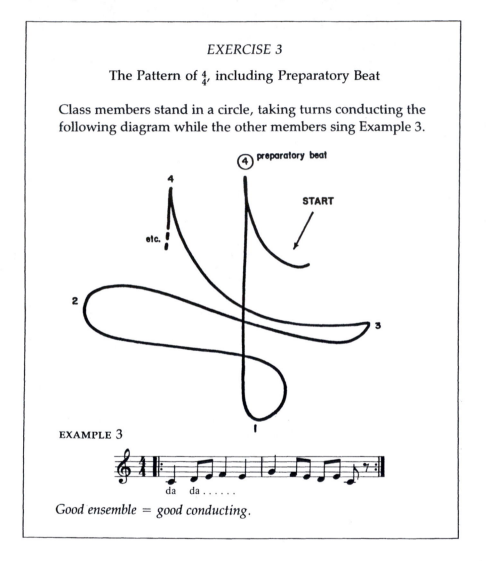

EXERCISE 3

The Pattern of $\frac{4}{4}$, including Preparatory Beat

Class members stand in a circle, taking turns conducting the following diagram while the other members sing Example 3.

EXAMPLE 3

da   da . . . . . .

Good ensemble = good conducting.

The Final Beat (Cut-off)

To understand the proper placement (within the conducting patterns) of the final beat or "cut-off" of a composition, you must realize that when you and the ensemble are on beat 1 of a given measure of music, you are at the *beginning of beat 1,* and that beat will last until the commencement of beat 2. Similarly, beat 2 does not end until beat 3 starts, and so on. With this in mind, therefore, if we consider the placement (within the pattern) of the final beat, it becomes very clear that you must always conduct an extra beat to "cut off" the final sound of a composition.

EXERCISE 4

The Pattern of $\frac{4}{4}$, including Cut-off

With class members standing in a circle, each student takes a turn conducting the diagram below, while the others sing Example 4.

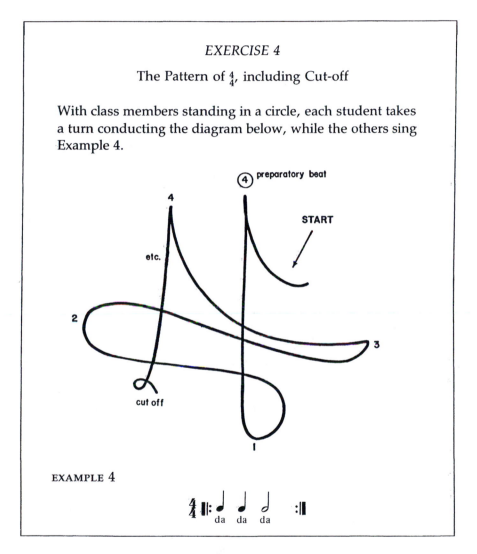

EXAMPLE 4

Suggested Repertoire: Mendelssohn, "He That Shall Endure to the End"
from *Elijah*
Saint-Saëns, *Ave Verum Corpus*

The Pattern of $\frac{3}{4}$

EXERCISE 5

The Pattern of $\frac{3}{4}$

A. The class practices conducting the pattern of $\frac{3}{4}$:

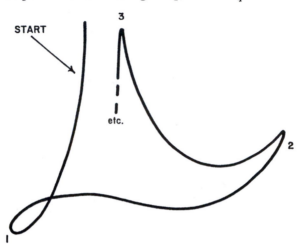

B. With class members standing in a circle, each student takes a turn conducting the diagram below while the others sing Example 5.

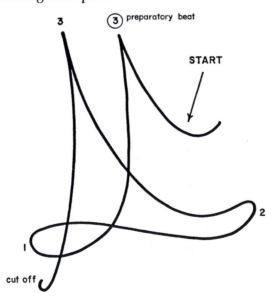

8

EXAMPLE 5

da   da   da . . . . .

Suggested Repertoire: Purcell, *Come, Ye Sons of Art*
Haydn, Agnus Dei from *Mass in C*

The Pattern of $\frac{2}{4}$

The pattern of $\frac{2}{4}$ is one of the hardest to conduct well, because an excessive rebound on the downbeat can be easily confused with the second beat.

EXERCISE 6

The Pattern of $\frac{2}{4}$

A. With class members standing in a circle, each student practices conducting the pattern of $\frac{2}{4}$ as illustrated in the diagram below, making sure not to rebound too high on the downbeat.

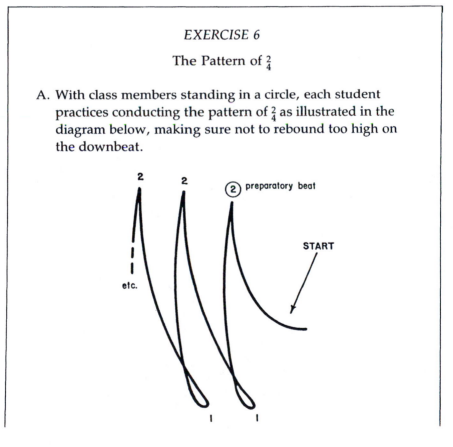

B. With class members standing in a circle, each student takes a turn conducting the diagram on p. 9 while the others sing Example 6.

EXAMPLE 6

doo doo doo . . . . . .

Suggested Repertoire: Marcello, *Maoz Tzur*
Ingalls, *Northfield*
Britten, *Jubilate Deo*

The Patterns of $\frac{4}{1}$, $\frac{4}{2}$, $\frac{4}{8}$, $\frac{4}{16}$, etc.

The conducting pattern used for the meters of $\frac{4}{1}$, $\frac{4}{2}$, $\frac{4}{8}$, $\frac{4}{16}$, and any other meter with a numerator of 4 is *identical with the pattern used for the meter of $\frac{4}{4}$.*

The Patterns of $\frac{3}{1}$, $\frac{3}{2}$, $\frac{3}{8}$, $\frac{3}{16}$, etc.

The conducting pattern used for the meters of $\frac{3}{1}$, $\frac{3}{2}$, $\frac{3}{8}$, $\frac{3}{16}$, and any other meter with a numerator of 3 is *identical with the pattern used for the meter of $\frac{3}{4}$.*

The Patterns of $\frac{2}{1}$, $\frac{2}{2}$, $\frac{2}{8}$, $\frac{2}{16}$, etc.

The conducting patterns used for the meters of $\frac{2}{1}$, $\frac{2}{2}$, $\frac{2}{8}$, $\frac{2}{16}$, and any other meter with a numerator of 2 is *identical with the pattern used for $\frac{2}{4}$.*

Changing Meters

Now that you have conducted patterns of 4, 3, and 2, it is time for you to practice changing from one pattern to another during the same selection.

EXERCISE 7

Changing Meters

Members of the class take turns conducting Examples 7a through 7d.

EXAMPLE 7a

doo doo doo . . . . . .

EXAMPLE 7b

doo doo doo . . . .

EXAMPLE 7c

doo doo   doo . . . . . .

EXAMPLE 7d

doo doo doo . . . . . .

Suggested Repertoire: Stravinsky, Sanctus from *Mass*

———, *Ave Maria*

Vaughan Williams, *O vos omnes*

Chapter Two

SCORE, VOICE, WARM-UP AND INTONATION

Score Preparation

The goal in studying a musical score, large or small, for conducting purposes, is to know it so well that it becomes part of you. At that point you have a clear idea of how the music will sound in performance. The time between the first rehearsal and the performance should be spent closing the gap between what happened during the first reading of the score by the chorus and your vision of what that performance should be, based on your thorough absorption of the music.

Many conductors of non–music-reading choral groups rarely study a score. They learn it while teaching the different vocal lines to their chorus. Except for the simplest pieces, this is a very antimusical process, since the conductor inevitably spends most of the rehearsal time on the difficult passages. The resulting performance focuses attention on these passages rather than on the composition as a whole.

There follows a marked score of Thomas Tallis's *If Ye Love Me*. I have chosen this composition to demonstrate how to study a score, because in addition to being a beautiful piece of music, it is accessible to almost any chorus.

Essentially a polyphonic work, it features more than one important idea at any given time. There are also some harmonic connotations which may help us decide which of two melodies that seem equally important deserves the focus of our attention.

PROCEDURE

1. Sight-sing each of the four parts.
2. Mark the spots where you had difficulty.
3. Mark the spots where you expect your singers to have difficulty.

4. Memorize the underlined parts as if they were one continuous vocal line from beginning to end.
5. Sing and conduct from memory that continuous line in front of a mirror.
6. Repeat Step 5 and add the following: look in the direction of each voice section at least two beats before the continuous line shifts to that section.
7. Repeat step 6 and incorporate a preparatory beat immediately preceding the assumption of the continuous line by each voice section. The preparatory beat should remain in the basic tempo of the piece but have a bouncier feel to it, much like the action of the diaphragm when a person is taking a breath.
8. Plan and practice left-hand movements that reflect the natural rise and fall of the different musical phrases.*
9. Repeat each step as necessary.

You might find that some of the steps outlined in this chapter are too difficult for you at this stage. Practice as many as you can and come back to this chapter periodically after you have worked through the material that follows.

THOMAS TALLIS, *If Ye Love Me, Keep My Commandments*

*For further study of left-hand movements, see Chapter Three, page 26.

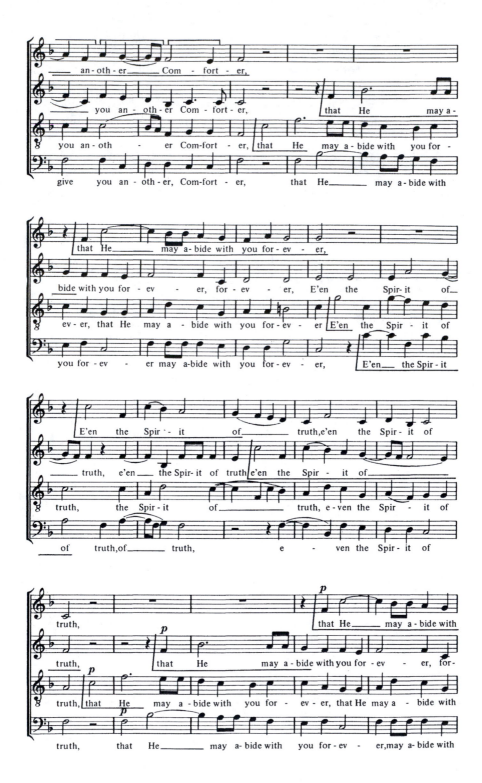

Score, Voice, Warm-Up, Intonation

Vocal Production

One of your major tasks as a choral conductor, especially with a non-professional chorus, is to cause that chorus to sing well. Before making specific suggestions on how to accomplish this, let me make some general observations about vocal training.

Between the years of 1961 and 1977, while serving as Director of Choral Music at the Juilliard School in New York, I held auditions for potential soloists with the Juilliard Chorus and Orchestra. Those auditions afforded me a rare opportunity to hear some very talented young singers who were studying with some excellent voice teachers. I heard some of these young people several times at intervals of a year or so, and I was able to follow their progress and evaluate the effects of their vocal training. Most of the time there was obvious progress, but occasionally I could detect vocal problems which had developed. In most of these cases there was immediate improvement when the student changed voice teachers. My conclusion was that while all the voice teachers were first-rate, not every teacher is good for every student. It is imperative that teacher and student are in close communication with each other and that the student has complete trust in the teacher.

The trust is necessary because when we sing we do not hear ourselves as the rest of the world hears us, but partially through the reverberations of our head bones. That fact is manifest when we listen to our recorded voice for the first time—"This is not me!" is a very common reaction.

I myself have studied voice with three different teachers at different times. While all three teachers were very good, I made the most progress under the tutelege of the one who communicated best with me.

What makes voice teaching so fragile is that voice teachers very often use abstractions and metaphors like: "Open your mouth as if you were biting an apple"; or "When you start to sing, think of a flower opening"; "Approach this note from above"; "Make this high note a little darker"; "Use more head resonance on this low note"; and so on.

Instrumental instruction, by comparison, tends to be much more pragmatic and down to earth, as, for example: "Try this phrasing, it might prove easier"; "Hold your bow at this angle"; "An alternate fingering for this same note would result in better intonation in this key"; etc.

In the numerous discussions I have had with many excellent singers and voice teachers concerning vocal production and the teaching thereof, I found that though they all seem to agree on what makes good singing, they express it in different ways.

My advice to you, the choral conductor, is: if at all possible, study voice privately, even if you do not intend to become a professional singer. Choose your teacher with great care and do not be satisfied until you find one with whom you communicate well and with whom you have the best rapport.

Before we discuss the many ways that the choral conductor can improve the vocal production of choral singers, let us review the fundamentals of good singing.

The voice is a wind instrument which produces sound by sending a column of air through the vocal cords (also called vocal folds, or membranes). The sound is then modified by resonating in the hollows of the neck, mouth, and nose.

Breath

The objective of breathing in singing is to maintain a well-regulated supply of air pressure for the production of sound. In order to accomplish this, "a full breath must often be taken very rapidly and then kept in a state of controlled compression for as long as 20 seconds." . . . "The

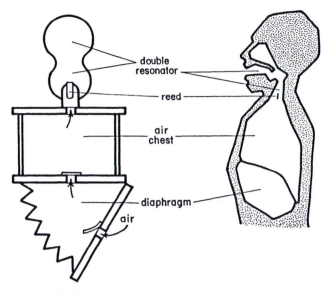

THE MECHANICS OF VOCAL PRODUCTION

largest amount of air can be inhaled by properly combined action of raising the ribs (costal breathing) and of contracting the diaphragm (diaphragmatic breathing). The latter has also been called 'abdominal' breathing from the fact that the diaphragm is hidden and evidence of its contraction is the protrusion of the abdominal wall, caused by lowering the roof of that cavity.'* By putting your hands on your waist and feeling the protrusion of the abdominal wall, you can verify if a deep breath was taken properly. A quick way of detecting incorrect breathing is by your singers' raised shoulders.

The importance of proper and adequate breathing cannot be overemphasized in choral singing. A singer who produces a note without proper breath support is like a tennis player who hits a ball without watching it. In tennis the result is most often a losing shot. In singing, it is an ugly sound and a sore throat. The less vocal training your singers have, the more often you will have to remind them to breathe.

Remember, however, that mere repetition of any instruction is the kiss of death in teaching. It is better to paraphrase! Alternative ways of saying the same thing will come to you naturally if you try to be specific in enumerating the reasons that singers fail to breathe properly.

*W. A. Aikin, M.D., "Singing," in *Grove's Dictionary of Music and Musicians* (London, 1945), p. 762.

Here are some alternative approaches you might come up with: "Write in a breath mark at the comma on measure 55"; "Since we are placing the final consonant of this phrase on the first eighth of the quarter-note rest, you must do your breathing rhythmically during the remaining eighth note"; "The only way you can stay in tune to the end of this phrase is to take a deeper breath at its commencement on measure 35"; or "We need much more breath for 'come, come, ye sons of arts, come, come away' because all of those aspirated consonants use a lot of air if pronounced properly."

As a conductor you should also remember that a *forte* passage will need more air than a *piano* passage; but the most deceptive phrase in terms of adequate breath is one that starts *piano* followed by a *crescendo*.

An awareness of the many reasons why singers do not breathe adequately, such as insufficient anticipation of the length of a musical phrase, expending too much air on a phrase attack, or preoccupation with the final consonant of the preceding phrase, should provide several different ways to remind them that the most fundamental component of good singing is *breath*.

Posture

I have started the discussion of vocal production with breath to emphasize its great importance to good singing. Good posture, however, is also vital for proper vocal production. When the chorus is standing, each singer's feet should be planted solidly on the ground with the weight centered. A seated chorus should have straight backs, relaxed shoulders, and uncrossed legs.

Things to Remember

At this point it is important to remind you that a chorus rehearsal is not a voice lesson. If you have taken voice lessons or taught voice yourself, you know how difficult it is to teach even on a one-to-one basis, so don't ever try to do it in a group. This should be avoided especially with a chorus of professional singers. Remember that most of them already have a voice teacher.

But don't despair: choral conductors have many other ways of affecting their singers' tone quality. As a matter of fact, the single element that most affects the eventual sound quality of a chorus in performance (or an orchestra, for that matter) is the actual conducting technique or physical movements of the conductor.

Score, Voice, Warm-Up, Intonation

If your arms are tense and strained, the singers will have a hard time following your motions and will eventually become tense themselves. They will therefore not breathe properly and their vocal passages will become constricted.

If your preparatory beats are not secure, flowing, and relaxed, the chorus cannot breathe properly before starting to sing and is therefore susceptible to vocal trouble.

If your beat pattern is not clear, some sections of the chorus will be confused by it and will sing hesitantly, another way of losing breath support.

Thus what you can do is study the score thoroughly and practice conducting in front of a mirror (making sure your intentions are as clear to your singers as they are to you).

Be sure that when you are cuing the individual sections of the chorus that those cues serve as good preparatory beats. At the same time be sure that your beat stays with the pattern so as not to confuse the other sections of the chorus. While doing all of this, be sure your conducting has a natural musical flow to it.

In short, don't lose sight of the forest while giving individual attention to the trees.

Other elements of conducting and rehearsing which affect the singing of your chorus will be discussed in later chapters, especially the section in Chapter Five, *Vowels and Vocal Production*.

Warm-up

It is essential that every rehearsal begin with a carefully controlled and regulated warm-up, but this cannot be achieved in five minutes. In fact, the entire session should be one long warm-up.

In order to accomplish this, the opening exercises must start in the low-middle vocal range and end in the high-middle range. Subsequent exercises can gradually reach toward the further extremes of the voice but must, under no circumstances, actually reach those extremes. High notes sung *pp* should not be included in a warm-up.

Bad intonation can often result when voices are "cold." In this case, the conductor should not be overly concerned, because poor intonation usually disappears with subsequent exercises.

In addition to warm-up exercises, it is advisable to sing a short piece of music that lies in the middle of the vocal range of all four voices. A good example is the final chorale of J. S. Bach's *Passion according to St. Matthew;* however, any comparable piece from the program in preparation will do.

The advantage of using a piece of music as part of the warm-up routine is that it affords the conductor the opportunity to combat boredom through musical interest. The problem of boredom is a very real one. When singers—especially in a group—go through very familiar warm-up exercises in a humdrum manner, there is always a danger that they will not breathe properly and will not even be aware that they are hurting their voices. Therefore, if a conductor uses the same exercises again and again, it is important that some variety be introduced into the routine. This can be done, for example, by changing the syllables on which they are sung from "mi, ma, mo, mu" to "peem, pam, pom, poom"; by adding *crescendo* and *diminuendo* to the same exercise; by having the group sing the exercise *staccato;* and so forth.

The following are some useful warm-up exercises:

WARM-UP NO. 1

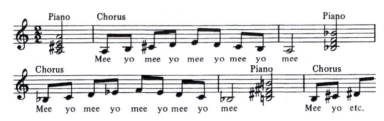

WARM-UP NO. 2

WARM-UP NO. 3

In addition to planning the rehearsal so that it can serve through-out as a warm-up, you must constantly listen to the chorus from the purely vocal point of view. Then, if the original plan of rehearsal does not work, and the voices start to sound strained, you must shift gears and rehearse another selection or another part of the composition which is less demanding vocally, or one with which the chorus is more familiar (a chorus is more likely to strain vocally when sight reading).

Intonation

Choral intonation is probably the single most misunderstood subject in the art of choral conducting.

The basic reason for this misunderstanding is that, unlike the other technical aspects of choral conducting (which most people can deal with rationally and unemotionally), the subject of intonation is laden with psychological overtones in which egos are involved.

For example, when a conductor stops a singer to point out a faulty rhythm, the singer will usually accept the criticism graciously and try to correct the mistake. However, when a conductor points to faulty into-nation with a statement such as "You are singing flat," the singer is very liable to take offense. This is probably due to the deep-seated notion that singing out of tune is synonymous with being unmusical. As a mat-ter of fact, I'd venture to say that most singers will interpret a comment like "You are singing flat" to mean, "You should not be in music." But anybody who knows anything about singing realizes that it is possible, even probable, that a singer with an excellent ear will sing flat or sharp as a result of faulty vocal production.

In fact, I have heard singers whom I know to possess absolute pitch sing "out of tune" due to vocal problems—come to think of it, I know several conductors with absolute pitch who almost invariably sing out of tune!

How the myth got started that "not being able to carry a tune" equates with "unmusical" is not the subject of this book, but the exis-tence of this equation in the minds of singers is germane to our subject. It is very important that the conductor not create anxieties for his singers in any form or fashion, because an anxious singer is one who is not breathing properly and will inevitably sing out of tune.

In order to deal with intonation problems effectively, one must first try to pinpoint the specific cause of the problem, then try to correct it. In the following paragraphs, we will touch on some of the most frequent causes of faulty intonation.

1. *Lack of Support.* Singing flat is most often due to insufficient breath support. The cure for this is: breathe!
2. *Ascending and Descending Intervals.* Sometimes one of the parts seems to go flat for no apparent reason. The explanation, very often, is the absence of that extra effort necessary to sing an ascending scale or any ascending interval, or the exaggerated relaxation which often occurs in singing a descending scale or any descending interval. In both cases, the most effective cure seems to be: sing *large intervals on the way up and small ones on the way down.*
3. *Singing Chromatic Passages.* Although the tempered scale has been in general use for more than two centuries, our ears still have not adjusted to it and we continue to prefer the natural intervals of the overtone series. (This is why having a "good ear" is not sufficient preparation for piano tuning.) This is also the reason that a group of singers with fairly good ears, singing a chromatic scale up or down, will not always arrive at the perfect octave after singing twelve semitones.

    When an intonation problem arises as a result of a chromatic progression of more than three semitones, *clarify the harmonic implication of each note for the singers;* require that they sing a "large" semitone between C and C♯ and a "smaller" semitone between C♯ and D; a larger semitone between F and F♯ and a smaller semitone between F♯ and G; a larger semitone between B♭ and B and a smaller one between B and C.

    This procedure works well for a descending scale also: a large semitone from B to B♭, followed by a small semitone from B♭ to A; a large semitone from F♯ to F, followed by a small one from F to E. This technique often improves intonation and helps singers keep a sense of tonality. This often coincides harmonically with "perfect" rather than "tempered" tuning of the vertical chords.
4. *High Note on a Difficult Vowel.* When singers have difficulty singing a high note, voice strain coupled with faulty intonation may result. The best remedy for such a situation is to ask the singers to *open their mouths, forming the widest circle possible with their lips.* The alteration of the vowel sound which may result from this procedure will not be objectionable because it is hard for the ear to distinguish vowel sounds in the high vocal ranges.
5. *Long Sustained Notes.* When one of the chorus sections (soprano, alto, etc.) has to sustain a note for several measures, it is pos-

Score, Voice, Warm-Up, Intonation

sible that they will sing it carelessly while waiting to move to the next note. This occurs because they are not aware that, at some point while sustaining their long note, they have run out of breath and are straining their vocal cords.

The suggestion that they stagger their breathing and never sing when out of breath may cure the problem. Another cure is to insert *crescendos* or *diminuendos*, or both, which correspond to the natural rise and fall of the composition as manifested in the other voices. If these *crescendos* and *diminuendos* contradict the intention of the composer, you can eventually eliminate them after making sure that the singers get into the good habit of supporting the long note and not just holding it.

6. *Too Many Repetitions of an* A Cappella *Selection during Rehearsals. A Cappella* selections often become progressively flattened in the course of repetitions. If this happens, instead of spotting the exact place and cause of the flattening and dealing with it, thus adding further repetitions of the selection, you should apply the oldest "trick of the choral conducting trade": *Perform the piece a half-step higher.* If, however, you anticipate the problem well in advance of the performance, you can remedy it beforehand by *rehearsing the piece a half step lower and then raising the pitch to the original key just before the performance.* When we routinely repeat an *a cappella* selection, some of the singers get into bad vocal habits because of the combination of particular notes with certain syllables. By raising pitch a half-step, we seem to "cut new grooves" vocally and the bad habits disappear.

If a great deal of repetition in rehearsing a particular *a cappella* piece is unavoidable, *keep varying the key in which you rehearse it,* going as much as a minor third above or below the original key.

7. *Low Notes.* Singers often use strained "chest" tones for low notes. A suggestion that they mix in "head resonance" or "head voice" improves the quality of sound and thereby improves intonation.

8. *Singing Sharp.* The main cause of pitch sharpening in choral singing is excessive tension and strain on the vocal cords, sometimes called "pushing." Some of the reasons why a chorus will push are:
   a. because the conductor is "pushing" or straining his arm muscles;

b. a passage is too high for the voices in question;

c. the singers are trying to sing too loud.

Obviously, in the first instance, the conductor must relax. In the second, vocal redistribution in the case of most parts is the answer. However, for the top voice, vowel modification can help. In the third case, the conductor must reassure the singers that pushing is self-defeating in terms of volume.

9. *How Conductors Can Cause Bad Intonation.* A conductor can cause his singers to sing with bad intonation without anyone, including himself, suspecting the reason. For example, an insecure cue to the tenor section may catapult most of the tenors into their vocal line without enough breath to last through the entire phrase, thereby guaranteeing faulty intonation.

A conductor who uses tense arm muscles will often cause singers to strain and "push" their vocal cords, thus causing a sharpening of the pitch. As to the matter of insecure cues, a conductor should learn the music thoroughly and practice the conducting motion appropriate for the cue in question.

Conclusion

As we can see from the problems examined in the foregoing pages, faulty intonation can be produced by a variety of causes, all of which have remedies. However, since the subject of intonation is such a sensitive one and involves the *amour propre* of the singer, *it is imperative that the conductor pinpoint specific causes of faulty intonation and apply the appropriate remedies.* Accusatory remarks like "You are flat," and "Can't you hear?" won't achieve the desired result. Insulting remarks make a chorus anxious. An anxious singer cannot breathe properly and a singer who does not breathe properly cannot sing in tune.

The exhortation "Listen to each other!" is useless because it makes no sense. What does it really mean? Should the singers who are singing in tune listen to the ones who are singing flat and adjust to them, or should the ones who are singing flat listen to the ones who are singing in tune? And how can the singers know to which of these groups they belong? Consider this: If you are singing flat in a chorus, are *you* going to know it?

Also consider the following phenomenon: most of the time when choruses go flat, they do so in harmony. In other words, a chorus which starts singing an *a cappella* piece in D major may end it together in perfect harmony in C♯ major. Sometimes the slide may be less than half a step down, to somewhere between D and C♯—a no-man's-land in the music of our Western culture. However, no matter where the singers end the piece, they seem to be in perfect harmony.

The question must arise: Could they ever finish in perfect harmony if they were not listening to each other? Therefore, *don't* say "Listen to each other!"—they *are* listening! Instead, do your job as a conductor and listen to *them;* then come up with specific solutions to the problems that have arisen. And until you are sure of exactly where the trouble is, it is better to say nothing.

Chapter Three

TEMPO FLUCTUATIONS, LEFT HAND

Accelerando and Ritardando

To achieve the effects of *accelerando* and *ritardando*, one must maintain a continuous *predictable* beat which gradually accelerates or decelerates (depending on the effect desired).

EXERCISE 8

$\frac{4}{4}$ + *Accelerando* + *Ritardando*

A. The class practices conducting the diagram below with gradual *acceleration* of the tempo.
B. The class practices conducting the diagram below with gradual *retardation* of the tempo.

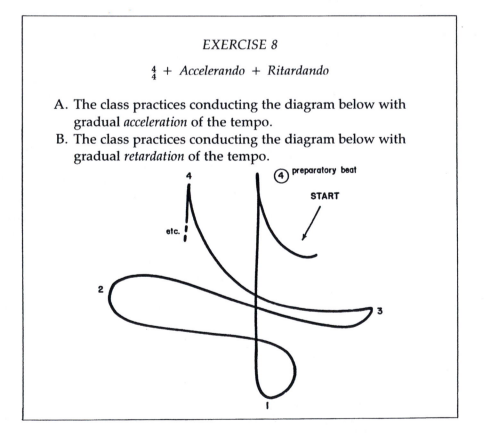

$\frac{4}{4}$ + *Accelerando* + *Ritardando*

In all exercises throughout this book, the same procedure is to be followed: with the class standing in a circle, each student takes a turn conducting the diagram with the rest of the class singing the example. This blanket instruction will hereafter be repeated only the first time it appears in each chapter, as a reminder. Only specific instructions pertaining to the exercise at hand will henceforth be given. This exercise, for example, is to be repeated twice: first with an *accelerando*, then with a *ritardando*.

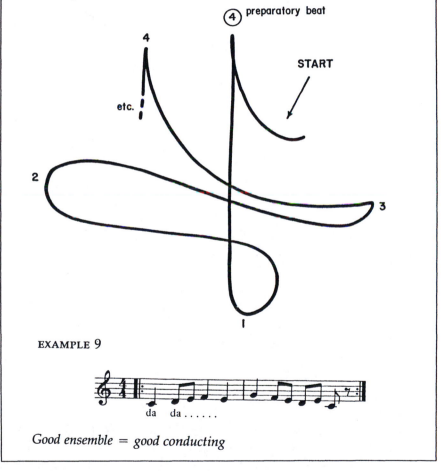

EXAMPLE 9

da   da . . . . . .

Good ensemble = good conducting

Suggested Repertoire: Tallis, *If Ye Love Me*

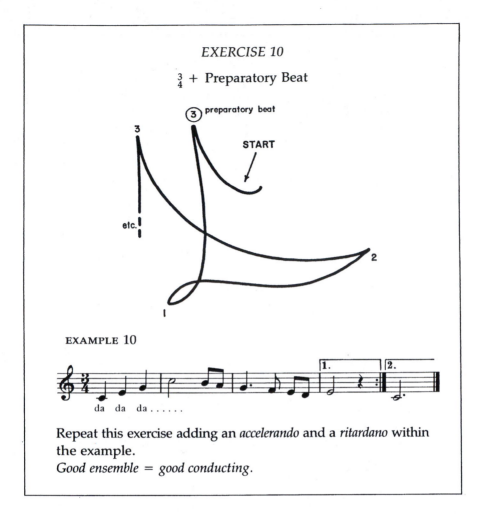

EXERCISE 10

$\frac{3}{4}$ + Preparatory Beat

EXAMPLE 10

Repeat this exercise adding an *accelerando* and a *ritardano* within the example.

Good ensemble = good conducting.

Suggested Repertoire: Weber, Gloria from *Mass in G Major*
Schubert, Kyrie from *Mass in G Major* (No. 2)
Dvořák, *Songs Filled My Heart* from *In Nature*
Purcell, *Come, Ye Sons of Art*

The Role of the Left Hand

While there is basic agreement on the functions of the right hand in conducting, the role of the left hand remains a matter of individual interpretation. As a matter of fact, many great masters of the baton have said that a conductor can accomplish practically everything with the right hand alone.

In this section I will try to summarize my observations on the best use of the left hand. Let me say at the outset: *the left hand should not mirror the right hand's beat*; in other words, what can be done well with one hand should not be done with two. This advice is given for a very practical reason: when a conductor beats time with both hands, the chances are that different parts of the ensemble (especially if it is a large group) will see a slightly different beat.

The following are some of the best uses for the conductor's left hand:

1. Indicating the exact growth of a *crescendo:* If a *crescendo* is to take place over four measures of music, for example, the actual growth in sound could assure an infinite variety of shapes, as illustrated below:

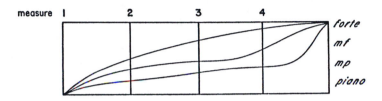

The left hand is the perfect instrument for indicating the shape of *crescendo* without the conductor saying a word.

2. Indicating the decline in volume of a *diminuendo:*

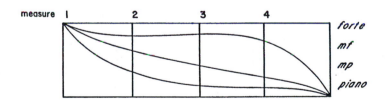

EXERCISE 11

A. $\frac{4}{4}$ + *Crescendo* and *Diminuendo* in Left Hand

Conduct four measures of $\frac{4}{4}$ with the right hand while moving the left hand straight up during the first two measures

---

and straight down during the last two measures. During the exercise, it is important to make sure that the left hand, while moving up and down, does not subtly beat time or veer to the side. The movement of the left hand must be smooth and devoid of any rhythm.

However, while practicing this exercise, in addition to moving the left hand up and down at a steady pace, the student should move it up and down at various speeds, reflecting perhaps the different *crescendos* and *diminuendos* illustrated in the diagrams below.

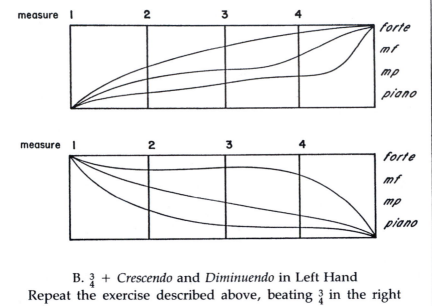

B. $\frac{3}{4}$ + *Crescendo* and *Diminuendo* in Left Hand

Repeat the exercise described above, beating $\frac{3}{4}$ in the right hand.

Training the Left Hand to Be Independent

While practicing Exercise 11, you must have observed how difficult it is to move the hands in truly independent fashion. Of the many exercises I have used during my twenty years of teaching, the ones that seem most useful for achieving the kind of hand independence essential to conductors are those described in Exercise 11. Further training is offered in Exercise 12.

EXERCISE 12

$\frac{3}{4}$ + Independent Left Hand

A. Repeat aloud the following rhythmic pattern:

one   two and three

while moving your hands simultaneously and quickly between the points indicated in the diagrams below.

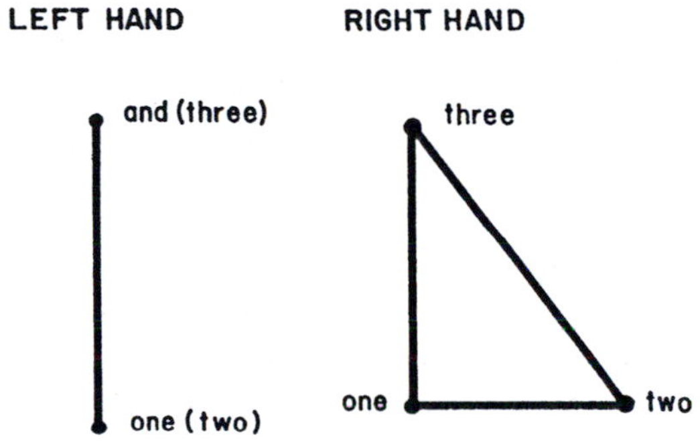

LEFT HAND   **RIGHT HAND**

B. Repeat the exercise above with the right hand moving smoothly (at an even pace) between one, two, and three while the left hand moves quickly between its points.
C. Repeat the exercise once again, but this time both hands are to move smoothly between their respective points.

N.B.: You may not be able to master Exercise 12 immediately. Keep practicing all the parts in rotation until you can do all three easily. If you have particular difficulty with Exercise 12C, come back to it after a few weeks when you have gained a little more experience in actual conducting.

Cuing

Cue a singer or instrument (or group of voices or instruments) for one of two basic reasons:

1. When, in your view, the entering voice represents the most important musical event at that moment and should receive the most attention from performers and audience (as is very often the case with most entrances of a subject in a fugue);
2. Because the performers need the cue for practical reasons. (E.g., the third trombone of the orchestra, after a rest of 237 measures, has to join a *tutti ff* chord of the brass section at measure 238. He has been counting those rests very conscientiously but would like to have the added assurance from the conductor that his count was right, lest he burst out with the right *forte* note at the wrong time.)

It is important that you, as the conductor, realize that cuing is only done for one of these two reasons. You must also be aware that because of their intrinsic differences, these two types of cues should be approached differently.

When cuing the entry of what is musically the most important musical line at a given time, one simply incorporates the cue into one's conducting in the manner to be discussed later in this chapter. However, when one has to cue for practical reasons, one must not only incorporate the cue into one's technique but must also do it in such a manner as to insure that the cue does not attract undue attention.* Otherwise, the entire concert will turn into a succession of traffic signals, while the musical content of the composition will be overlooked by everyone.

When cuing involves an important musical line, as in Example 13 below, you should conduct preparatory beats where indicated and, in conjunction, point with the left hand in the direction of the appropriate section. This is one of the occasions when the left hand can mirror the rhythm (but not the pattern) of the right hand.

EXERCISE 13

Cuing

Conduct the following patterns for the right and left hand at measure 8 of Example 13.

---

*This is one of the cases where eye contact with the third trombonist two or three beats prior to such an entrance is most appreciated by the players.

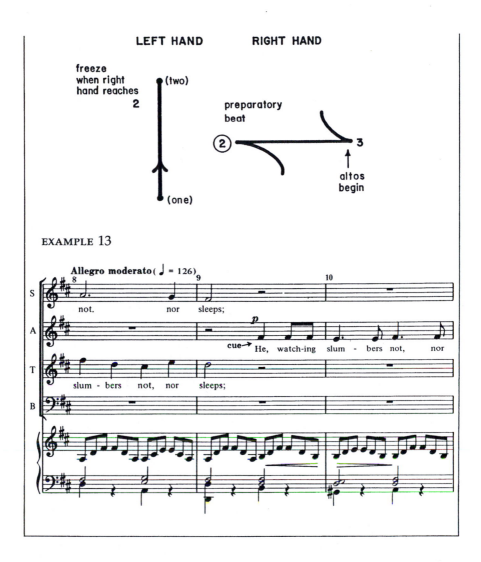

EXAMPLE 13

Suggested Repertoire: Mendelssohn, "Blessed are the men who fear Him" from *Elijah*

In this and most similar instances, I personally prefer a left hand pointing at the altos, starting gently, approximately on the fourth beat of the preceding measure and leaving the actual cuing process to the right hand alone, thus eliminating altogether the motion indicated in Exercise 13.

Cuing for practical reasons is much more subtle because it has to be done in a clear, efficient, but unobtrusive manner. At measure 77 of the same piece you must cue in the orchestra while maintaining the peaceful mood of the word "sleeps" and without drawing undue attention to the orchestra's entrance. In this particular case, eye contact with the orchestra a beat or two before it enters and a gentle preparatory beat on the fourth count of measure 76 will serve the chorus well when it starts the word "sleeps." It will also allow the orchestra to enter softly and in perfect ensemble.

MENDELSSOHN, *"He, watching over Israel"* from *Elijah*

Finally, in cuing for practical reasons, one must remember that if a choice has to be made between cuing a solo voice and cuing a group of voices that follow each other on successive beats, preference should be given to cuing the group of voices (or instruments). It is easier for a solo voice to fit into the ongoing texture than for a group which requires a cue that will also unify the section rhythmically.

The most important principle to remember when cuing for purely practical reasons is that the cuing motion must be placed within the framework of continuous musical conducting.

Chapter Four

MORE ABOUT CONDUCTING PATTERNS

Fermata (Hold)

When a *fermata* (⌢) occurs at the end of a musical composition (as in the example on p. 34), stop all movement, or hold still on the beat bearing the fermata. After a suitable length of time, raise your hand gently and conduct an additional downbeat for a cut-off as in the following diagram:

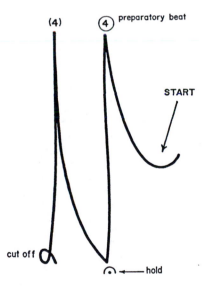

When there is a fermata in the middle of a composition and a continuous musical performance is desired (as in Example 14 on p. 36), resume conducting after the stop on the beat bearing the fermata.

EXERCISE 14

$\frac{4}{4}$ + ⌒ on Count 3

Members of the class take turns conducting the following diagram:

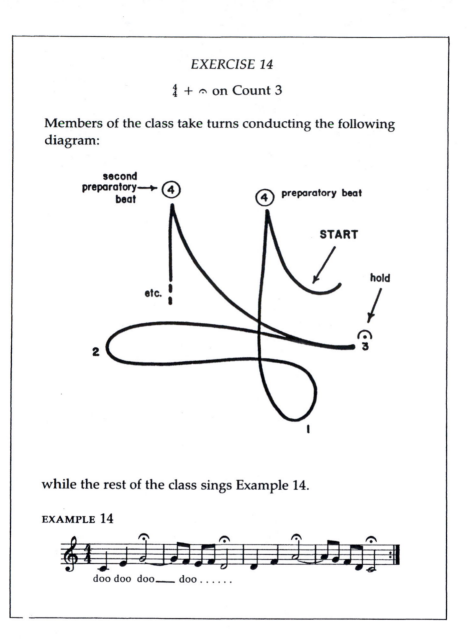

while the rest of the class sings Example 14.

EXAMPLE 14

doo doo doo___ doo . . . . . .

Suggested Repertoire: J. S. Bach, Chorale *Jesu meine Freude*, BWV 227
———— "O Haupt voll Blut und Wunden" from *St. Matthew Passion*
Elgar, *Go, Song of Mine*, Op. 57

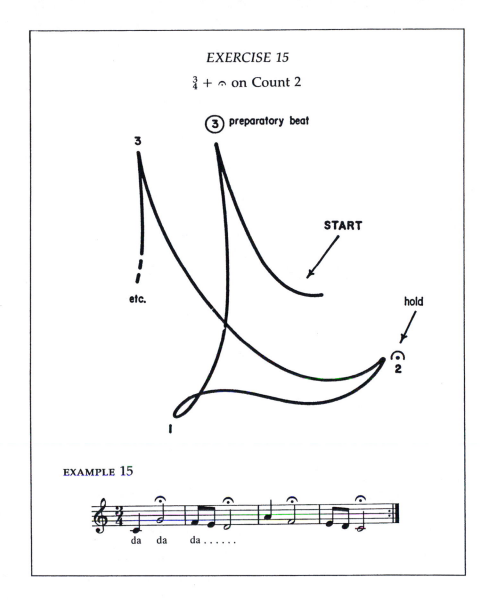

EXERCISE 15

¾ + ⌒ on Count 2

③ preparatory beat

3

START

etc.

hold

⌢
2

|

EXAMPLE 15

da   da   da......

Suggested Repertoire: J. S. Bach, Chorale *Des Heil'gen Geistes riche Gnad*
————, Chorale *O Herzensangst*
Haydn, Agnus Dei from *Mass in C (Paukenmesse)*

When a fermata occurs on a quarter note in the middle of a composition and continuous musical performance is desired, it is necessary to repeat the beat on which the fermata appears as a preparatory.

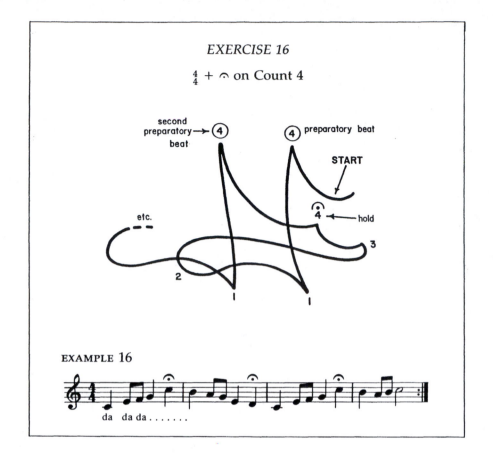

EXAMPLE 16

da da da.......

Close examination of the diagram above will reveal that the fourth beat (with the ⌢) is shortened in order to allow room for the repeat of the fourth beat as a preparatory.

Suggested Repertoire: J. S. Bach, Chorale *Jesu der du meine Seele*

——————, Chorale *Ach wie flüchtig, ach wie nichtig*

More about Conducting Patterns

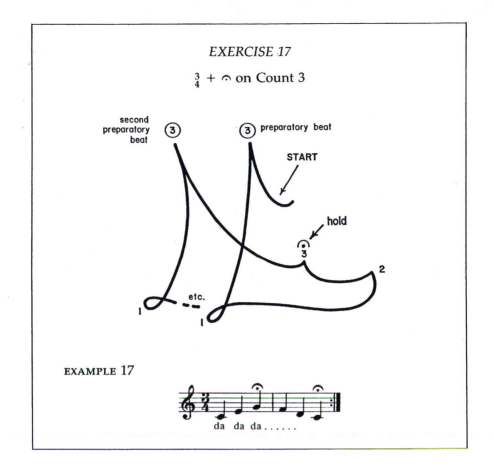

EXERCISE 17

$\frac{3}{4}$ + ⌒ on Count 3

EXAMPLE 17

da da da . . . . . .

Suggested Repertoire: Schubert, Credo from *Mass in B♭*

When there is a fermata on a whole note ⌒ in $\frac{4}{4}$ and the next moving note is on the downbeat of the next measure, the *second and third beats may be omitted* and the fourth beat used as a preparation for the next downbeat. (See diagram on page 40.)

Fermata   39

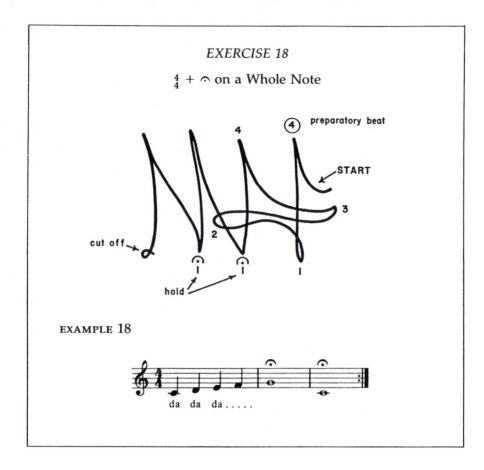

EXERCISE 18

$\frac{4}{4}$ + ⌢ on a Whole Note

preparatory beat

START

cut off

hold

EXAMPLE 18

da da da . . . . .

Suggested Repertoire: Bach, "Gloria sei dir gesingen from *Wachet auf,* *ruft uns die Stimme,* BWV 140
Schubert, Agnus Dei from *Mass in B♭*

More about Conducting Patterns

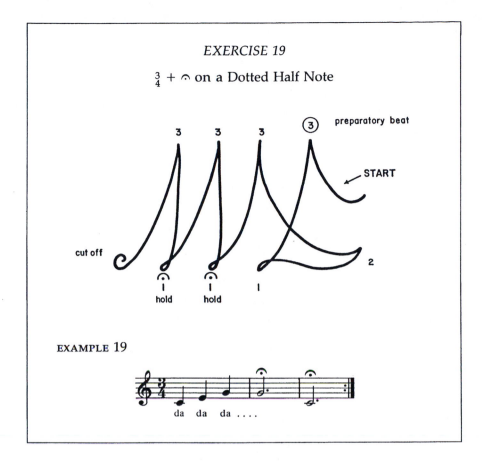

EXERCISE 19

$\frac{3}{4}$ + ⌒ on a Dotted Half Note

EXAMPLE 19

Suggested Repertoire: J. S. Bach, Chorale "Freu dich sehr" from *Wachet! betet! betet! wachet!* BWV 70

When there are fermatas on different beats (and in different voices) of the same measure, the last ⌒ should be held, as illustrated on p. 42:

BACH, *St. Matthew Passion*, no. 78

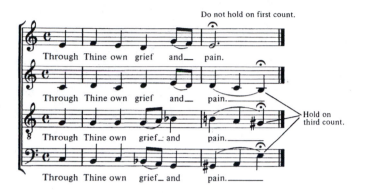

In the last measure of the example above, the *third* beat with the fermata is the one to be held. Beats one and two should be conducted as if there were no fermata. In the example below, we follow the same procedure:

MENDELSSOHN, *"Cast Thy Burden Upon the Lord"* from *Elijah*

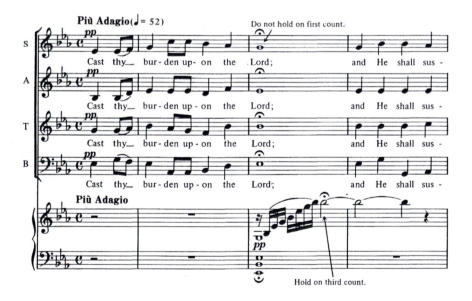

Suggested Repertoire: Mendelssohn, "Cast Thy Burden" from *Elijah*

More about Conducting Patterns

Beats that May Be Omitted

Any beat may be omitted except the downbeat. *Never omit a downbeat.* The diagrams on pages 40 and 41 demonstrate that certain beats may be omitted when a fermata is involved. One can also omit beats on which there is no rhythmical movement at all.

In the example below, there is no reason to beat out the second and third beats of the first measure. The fourth beat, however, has to be indicated to insure good ensemble on the downbeat of the second measure. Since there is no fermata in the first measure of the example, you must keep count of the second and third beats in your head.

VICTORIA, *O Magnum Mysterium*

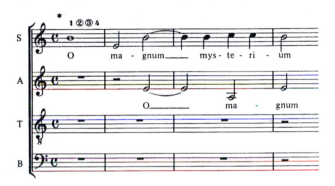

Suggested Repertoire: Tallis, *If Ye Love Me*

Even when a downbeat lacks rhythmic motion you must indicate it (see example on p. 44). The reason for this is that the musicians in the orchestra—who have only their own parts before them—will suddenly see, after their downbeat, a preparation for a third beat and will have no way of knowing that a whole measure has passed. Therefore the edict: *Never omit a downbeat!*

*Do not beat counts 2 and 3.

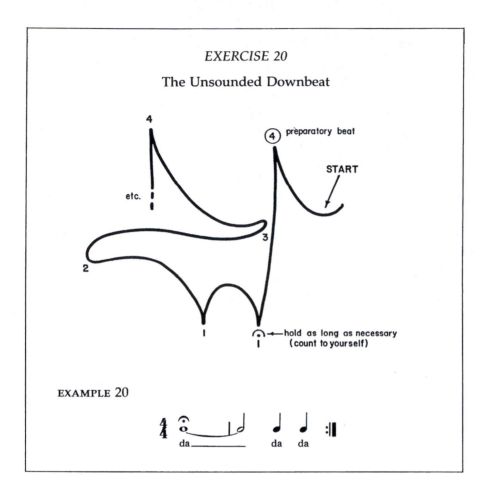

EXERCISE 20

The Unsounded Downbeat

4

(4) prèparatory beat

START

etc.

3

2

1

⌢ ← hold as long as necessary
1   (count to yourself)

EXAMPLE 20

$\frac{4}{4}$ 𝄻 da_____ da da :𝄇

Suggested Repertoire: Handel, "He was cut off from the land of the living" from *Messiah*

Starting on Various Beats of the Measure

Even when the music starts on any beat other than the first one, *the preparation always takes place on the preceding beat.*

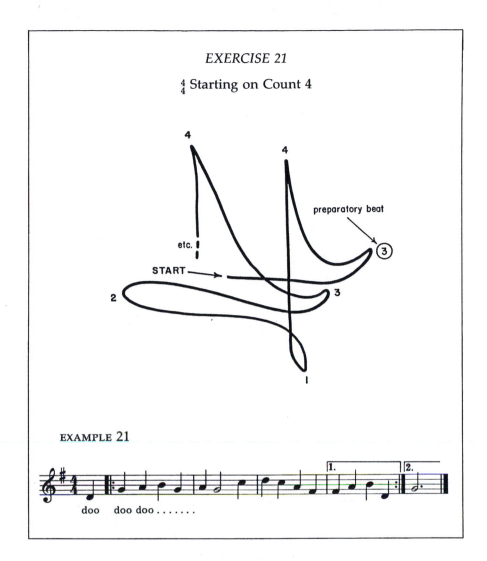

EXERCISE 21

$\frac{4}{4}$ Starting on Count 4

EXAMPLE 21

Suggested Repertoire: Bach, "O Haupt voll Blut und Wunden" from
St. Matthew Passion
Fauré, *Cantique de Jean Racine*

EXERCISE 22

$\frac{4}{4}$ Starting on Count 4 + ⌒.

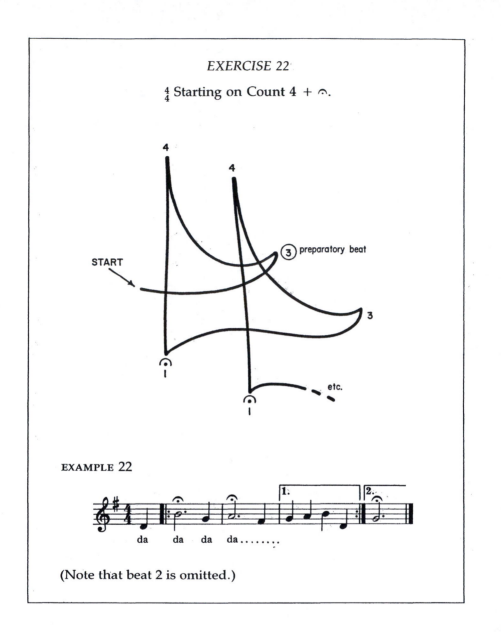

EXAMPLE 22

da   da   da   da.........

(Note that beat 2 is omitted.)

More about Conducting Patterns

EXERCISE 23

$\frac{4}{4}$ Starting on Count 4 and Omitting Beat 2

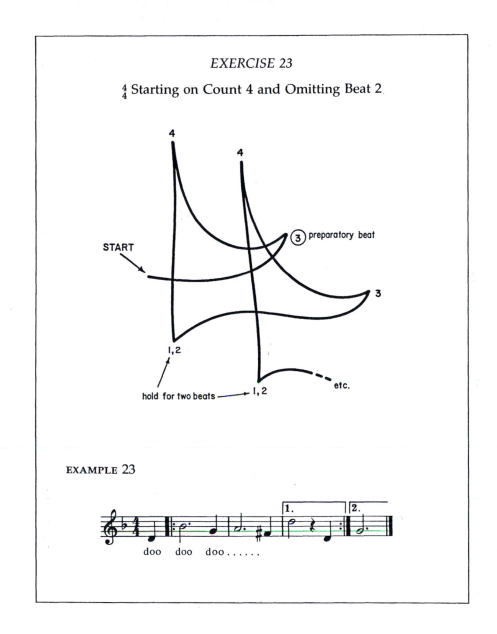

EXAMPLE 23

doo   doo   doo . . . . . .

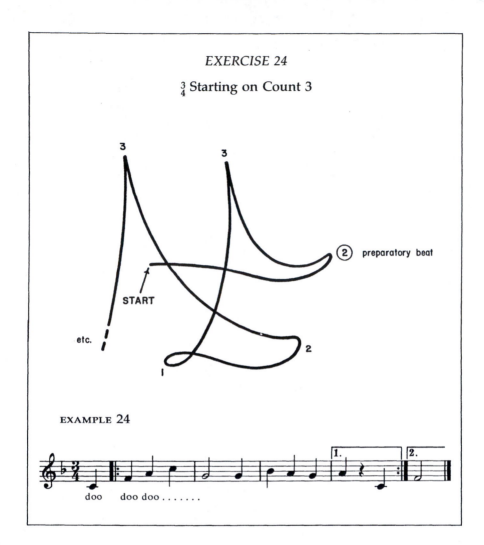

EXERCISE 24

¾ Starting on Count 3

EXAMPLE 24

doo   doo doo . . . .

Suggested Repertoire: Bloch, *O May the Words*

More about Conducting Patterns

EXERCISE 25

⁴⁄₄ Starting on Count 3

EXAMPLE 25

doo doo doo . . . .

Suggested Repertoire: W. L. Dawson, *There Is a Balm in Gilead*

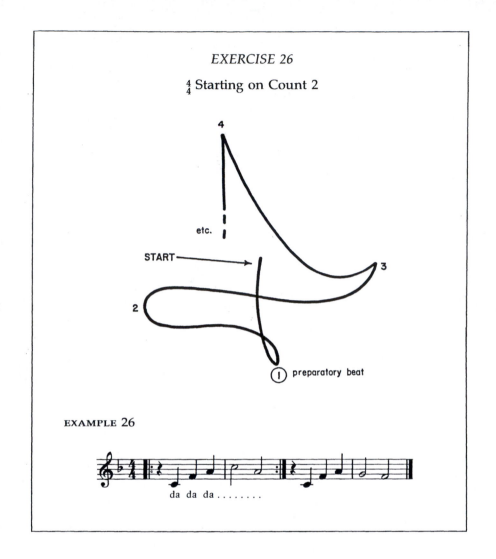

EXERCISE 26

¼ Starting on Count 2

4

etc.

START ⟶

3

2

① preparatory beat

EXAMPLE 26

da da da........

Suggested Repertoire: Handel, "He Trusted in God," "Worthy Is the Lamb," and "Since by Man Came Death" from *Messiah*

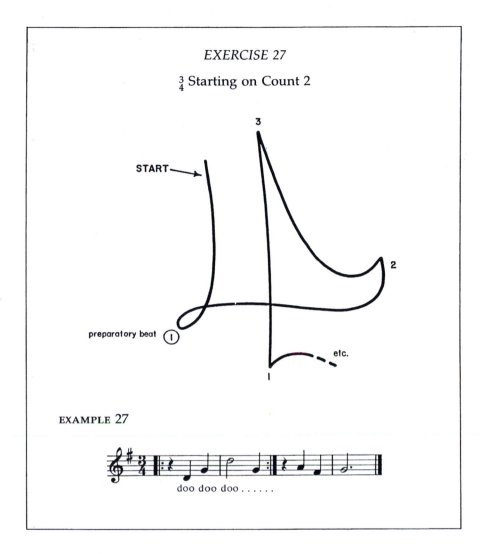

EXERCISE 27

¾ Starting on Count 2

EXAMPLE 27

doo doo doo . . . . . .

Suggested Repertoire: Stravinsky, Sanctus from *Mass*
                     Handel, "And the Glory of the Lord" from
                     Messiah

The following exercise will summarize the materials covered thus far in Chapter Four.

EXERCISE 28

Summary

Choose the appropriate beat patterns and conduct the following examples, taking turns as you have done in earlier exercises.

EXAMPLE 28A

da da da   da . . . . . .

EXAMPLE 28B

da da da   da . . . .

EXERCISE 29

$\frac{2}{4}$ Starting on Count 2

Take turns conducting each of the music examples using the beat pattern below.

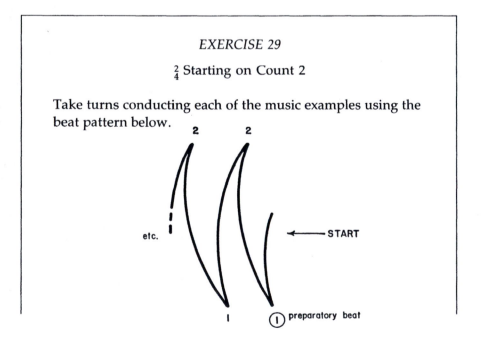

etc.

START

preparatory beat

More about Conducting Patterns

EXAMPLE 29A

da   da da . . . .

EXAMPLE 29B

doo doo doo doo doo . . . .

Suggested Repertoire: Britten, *Jubilate Deo*
French Folk Dance, *O Beautiful Young Maiden*
Dvořák, *O Here's a Day* from *In Nature*
Mendelssohn, "Lord How Thine Ear" from *Elijah*
Stravinsky, *Symphony of Psalms*

Rehearsing Slow Music

The major difficulty in performing slow music lies in the fact that the singers must sustain long phrases, breathe properly, and pace their expenditure of breath over the long phrases. This difficulty is exacerbated in rehearsal, where this sustaining effort has to be repeated every time the piece is rehearsed.

To minimize the problem, rehearse the piece at a moderate, comfortable tempo and, as you get closer to performance time, slow down to the desired tempo. Alert the singers to the extra breath required to sustain a slower tempo and use preparatory beats that are conducive to correct breathing: a preparatory beat in which the movement of the arm muscle resembles the movement of another muscle, the diaphragm.

Rehearsing Fast Music

If possible, rehearse fast music in tempo to preserve the correct duration of the musical phrases. If, however, the chorus is incapable of reading the music and text at the desired tempo, start rehearsing at a moderate, manageable tempo and in subsequent readings speed up the pace until the desired tempo is reached.

While rehearsing fast music at a slower tempo, some problems not inherent to the performance may appear. For example, the singers may breathe in the middle of phrases. Do not bother to correct them; most of these problems will disappear once you have brought the piece up to tempo.

You can speed up the process of learning a fast-moving piece of music by asking the chorus to recite the text in rhythm, then read the music on a syllable such as "da" or "doo," and finally combine music and text.

Chapter Five

DICTION

Communicating the Meaning of the Text

A singer with good diction can make listening to a song an effortless and enjoyable experience. Listening to a singer with bad diction is another matter. It is not uncommon to hear, in the middle of a sacred composition, pronouncements like: "Braise the Lord with songs of choy," or during a tender love song, "I laugh you". The need to avoid such incongruities is only one of several reasons we should strive for good diction in vocal music.

Vocal music is a finely balanced amalgam of two forms of human communication: language and music. While music is a natural, intuitive form of human expression (a baby does not have to be taught which sounds to make when it is sad or happy), language is an arbitrary creation of the human brain. Thus we find that the sound of words meaning certain things or arousing certain feelings in one language leave those who do not know that language completely unmoved.

It is this uneasy marriage between language and music that makes the attainment of text intelligibility a more subtle subject than the mere e-nun-ci-a-tion of ev'-ry word.

Let us see how some of the great composers have treated language.

J. S. Bach

J. S. Bach is often criticized as a composer who did not pay attention to the text and superimposed it rather carelessly on his music. However, a close examination of Bach's tremendous vocal output reveals that while he does not necessarily set every word perfectly, he never fails to set the *important words* to their best advantage, thus drawing attention to the meaning of the text as a whole rather than the single word.

An example of this can be heard in the *St. Matthew Passion* with the words "In three days I will rise again." The setting starts with the basses of the second chorus singing a rising scale of four notes. The tenors then enter, continuing the upward-moving scale for four more notes. The same procedure is repeated with each of the eight voices of this magnificent double chorus.

This seemingly endless rising scale associated with the words "In three days, I will rise again" makes such an indelible impression on the listeners that by the time all the voices have entered, a clear image of an endless ladder reaching to the heavens has been established.

Bach gives further emphasis to those important words by continuing the scales after the text moves on. Thus the listener cannot help but continue to see the heavenly ladder even after the text has progressed to other words which are less visually oriented.

Igor Stravinsky

In 1968 I prepared the Camerata Singers for a performance with the New York Philharmonic of Stravinsky's *Swesdalikij (Le Roi des etoiles)*. In advance, I studied the Russian text with several experts in the language. There was, however, one line of the poem which no one seemed to understand. Upon seeing Maestro Stravinsky a few weeks later, I asked if he could explain that one line to me. His startling reply was that he had never understood it himself. When he saw the bewildered look on my face he explained that when he liked a poem and decided to set it to music, he didn't care about the meaning of each sentence. For him, the meaning of the text as a whole is what mattered, and the words became musical building blocks.

Felix Mendelssohn

In his oratorio *Elijah* we find numerous examples of Mendelssohn's intention to point out (in this particular work) that soft is superior to loud and gentility stronger than bombast.

He does all of this through brilliant settings of words. For example, in the chorus "Behold, God the Lord passed by" we hear incredibly spectacular choral settings depicting mighty winds, earthquake, and fire. However, the climax of this piece happens later in a sublime setting of the words "and after the fire there came a still small voice, and in that still voice onward came the Lord."

In the chorus "He watching over Israel slumbers not nor sleeps," a *subito p* appears on the word "slumbers" in the final statement of this sentence in the exposition.

These are but three examples of the ways great composers find to highlight and draw attention to the meaning of a key word, an important sentence, or the whole text. Study the devices the great masters used to communicate the meaning of a text to an audience and use what you have learned. You can also use this knowledge to change a translation when you find that the translator did not do justice to the original by not keeping key words in musically advantageous places.

Remember, however, the most important principle: in vocal music we communicate the meaning of the text by drawing the audience's attention to the *most important* words through clear and correct diction (the details of which will be discussed in this chapter) and through musical devices.

Uniformity of Sound and Good Vocal Production

When singing all music (except folksongs) we should strive for a standard pronunciation, free of any regional dialects. Good diction is of paramount importance in achieving uniformity of sound, especially in choral music.

Before you start instructing your singers in the unification of their linguistic sounds, you must know the correct sounds of the language you are using. A correct, relaxed pronunciation of vowels and consonants is also the key to a good and unconstricted vocal production.

English Diction

Several excellent books have been written on English diction for the stage, and I recommend that you study at least one of them thoroughly.* Most of the advice given to the solo singer in a good diction book can be applied to choral singing as well. Some of it, however, must be modified before it can be applied to a chorus. It is these applications to the unique needs of the chorus which will be our main concern in the next few pages.

Vowels and Consonants: Sounded, Not Spelled

In our discussion of the correct pronunciation of words and how to connect them with other words in the same musical phrase, we will concern ourselves with actual sound rather than spelling.

*My own personal favorite is Madeleine Marshall's *The Singer's Manual of English Diction* (G. Schirmer). It is written by a superb musician.

Thus, the word "universe" starts with the consonant "y"—
"Yuniverse." The word "know" starts with the sound of "n," and the
word "honor" with a vowel sound.

Vowels

Uniformity of correct vowel sounds in choral singing can be attained if
you train your ear to differentiate between the many similar vowel sounds
which the English language employs. When the singers in your chorus
seem to disagree on the correct pronunciation of a certain vowel or insist
on pronouncing vowels with a regional inflection, it is time for you to
step in and ask for the proper vowel sound.

In the sentence "My father sat on the sofa all day," the letter "a"
has five different pronunciations. Therefore, it is necessary to have a
tool that assigns each sound one symbol regardless of spelling. This
excellent tool is the International Phonetic Alphabet. You do not have to
memorize it, but if you refer to it often in your studies and rehearsals
you will save yourself a lot of time and grief.

The IPA will also facilitate teaching your chorus correct pronunciation in languages other than English. All identical sounds, regardless
of the originating language, are represented by the same symbol.

International Phonetic Alphabet: Vowels

Symbol	Key Word	Symbol	Key Word
		DIPHTHONGS	
[a] or [a:]	father	[aɪ]	mine
[ɛ] or [e]	men	[ɛɪ]	pray
[ɪ]	it	[ɔɪ]	toy
[i]	seal	[aʊ]	now
[æ]	man	[ou]	rope
[u] or [u:]	too	[ɛə]	hair
[ʊ]	took	[ɪə]	near
[o]	ordain (unstressed)	[ɔə]	core
[ɔ] or [ɔ:]	fall	[ʊə]	sure
[ɜ] or [ə:]	yearn	TRIPHTHONGS	
[ʌ]	much	[aɪə]	ire
[ə]	gracious (unstressed)	[aʊə]	our

Study the vowel sounds and their correct pronunciation, remembering
that we are aiming to reproduce a standard English pronunciation free
of regional dialect.

Diphthongs and Triphthongs

When you sing a diphthong or a triphthong on a long note, sustain the first vowel sound for most of the duration of the note and then complete the diphthong, (or triphthong):

Thus → Night and day
should be sung: n[ɑ———ɪ]t and d[ɛ———ɪ]

and → This is our life
should be sung: [ɑ———ʊə]l[ɑ———ɪ]fe

Vowels and Vocal Production

Sing a long note in the middle of your range starting with the vowel sound [a] and move gradually through [ɛ] [ɪ] until you reach [i].

Sing: [ɑ]‾‾→ [ɛ] [ɪ]‾‾→ [i]

Observe the following phenomena: when you start singing [ɑ] your "jaw will be open at least an inch between your front teeth. The tongue lies flat upon the floor of the mouth . . . the base of the tongue is flat enough to make the back of the throat visible from the front . . . the neck is fully expanded by the combined action of holding the head erect, the ribs raised. . . . This position has the form of a double resonator with two principal resonance chambers (neck and mouth) uniting in the middle at right angles, where they are joined by a third accessory chamber, the nose."*

The position of the mouth when singing [ɑ] in the most comfortable part of your range—approximately a fifth above your lowest note) is such that the whole passage is open and expanded to the fullest extent.

When you change the vowel gradually from [ɑ] to [ɛ] to [ɪ] to [i], you raise and advance the entire tongue, which has reached an extreme position on the vowel [i]. When this vowel is sung on a high note it can cause a singer to block the passage of air through the resonators, resulting in an ugly constricted sound. Your solution is to change the vowel sound into the more open position [ɑ] [ɛ] [ɪ] [i].

You don't have to change all the way to [ɑ]. Settle on the sound closest to [i]—it can be a vowel sound which is between [ɪ] and [i].

*"Singing," *Grove's Dictionary of Music and Musicians*, 5th ed., ed. Eric Blom (London, 1945), p. 766.

When we move from the basic sound of [ɑ] in the direction of [u]—
[ɑ] [ɔ] [o] [ʊ] [u]—the tongue stays in its original position but the space between the lips becomes smaller until you form a very small circle on the sound [u].

If your singers seem to strain when the [u] sound falls on a high note, remind them that their lips forming the small circle should be relaxed and the opening inside their mouth (behind the lips) should be as wide as possible. If that suggestion does not alleviate the problem, modify the vowel sound by moving in the direction of [ɑ] [ɛ] [o] [ʊ] [u].

The change of the vowel should be as small as possible, just enough to open the resonating passages and restore good vocal production.

Consonants

Approximately half the consonants in the English language require the use of the vocal cords when they are spoken. The rest can be whispered (or aspirated).

Most vocalized consonants have equivalent aspirated consonants and vice versa. For example, if you whisper a "d" you will get a "t" and if you vocalize a "t" you will get a "d."

On the facing page is a table of all consonants vocalized and aspirated, arranged in pairs. Remember that most singing is done on the vowels. The consonants are used as connecting transitions between vowels.

Legato Singing

Within a musical phrase we sustain the vowels of each syllable for the full duration of the note. Therefore, if one word (or syllable) ends with a consonant and the following starts with a vowel, we sing the final consonant of the first word (or syllable) as a beginning of the following syllable.

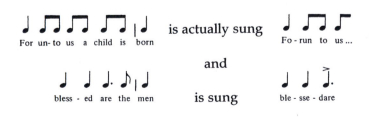

International Phonetic Alphabet: Consonants

VOCALIZED		ASPIRATED	
Symbol	*Key Word*	*Symbol*	*Key Word*
[b]	bell	[p]	play
[d]	doll	[t]	tree
[g]	good	[k]	king, cat
[l]	live		no equivalent
[m]	mother		no equivalent
[n]	night		no equivalent
[ŋ]	song		no equivalent
[r]	right		no equivalent
[v]	victory	[f]	free
[w]	one	[hw]	when
[j]	yellow		no equivalent
[z]	zebra, reason	[s]	song
[ʒ]	measure	[ʃ]	shine
[dʒ]	gentle, jingle	[tʃ]	church
[ð]	there	[θ]	three
	no equivalent	[h]	heaven

When a syllable begins and ends with a consonant the preceding vowel is still fully sustained: "no joy in mud-ville" is sung "no joy in mu-dville," and "ri-seth light" is sung "ri-se-thlight."

Exceptions

1. When [m], [n], and [ŋ] are preceded by a vowel, shorten that vowel somewhat and start the [m], [n], or [ŋ] on the pitch of the previous syllable: "Blessed are the m-en who fear him," not "the men", "All the n-ight," not "All the night"; and "Sing unto the Lord," not "Si-ng u-nto the Lord."
2. When [v] is between vowels and the pitch changes, sing the [v] on the lower pitch:

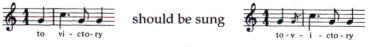

should be sung

and

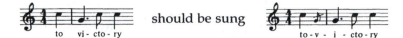 should be sung

When [v] is followed by a consonant sing the [v] on the note of the previous syllable:

When [v] is between vowels on the same pitch, sing the [v] on the first syllable:

3. If [l] is preceded by a vowel, sing the [l] on the first syllable as in

I   we_l·come you

If [l] is followed by a word beginning with a vowel, start that word with the [l]:

fall up - on them   should be sung   fa · lu - pon them

If [l] is preceded by a vowel and the next word commences with an [l], both should be pronounced thus:

pale look   should be sung   pa - le look

4. [w] can act as a consonant or a vowel. When it is a consonant it commences with a short oo [u] sound. In singing, when [w] is preceded by a vowel, the [u] sound can be started on the previous pitch:

the won - der of ....   should be sung   the_oo - on - der of ... ..

Special care must be taken not to carry the [u] sound to the next pitch.

*Double "l" is sung as a single "l."

The [u] sound of [w] should also start on the previous pitch when preceded by [l], [m], [n], or [ŋ]:

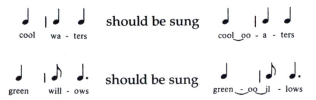

When [w] is preceded by any other consonant, **the [u] sound is not anticipated and is sung on the pitch where it is printed:**

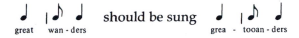

5. **Wh = [hw]—Words that begin with wh should be treated as if they commence with the letter h.**

Final Consonants (Before a Rest)

The diction problem most frequently encountered by the choral conductor is the placement of final consonants—consonants which are followed by rests.

Generally, final consonants should be sung at the end of the note under which they appear (see examples below). Make sure that the final consonant is always softer than the sound which precedes it.

VICTORIA, *O Vos Omnes*

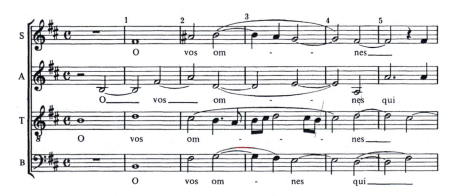

Soprano m.6 reads:

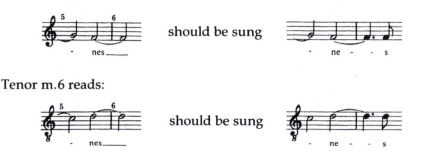

should be sung

Tenor m.6 reads:

should be sung

HANDEL, "And The Glory of The Lord" from *Messiah*

M.17 in soprano, alto, and bass reads:

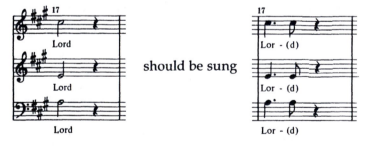

should be sung

Since composers do not, by and large, consider final consonants when notating their music, it is up to the choral conductor to determine the composer's musical intention and make a judgment on the placement of the final consonant accordingly.

In the Mendelssohn example below, it is clear that the soprano line is supposed to end before the tenors repeat the musical idea. Therefore,

Diction

the "ps" (of sleeps) should be placed either on the final eighth-note or quarter-note portion of the sopranos' whole note. Since the metronome marking is ♩ = 126 and the harmonic rhythm of the piece is progressing in half notes, placement of a double final consonant on the last eighth note would create ensemble problems (please refer to the section on double final consonants in this chapter). The double consonant will probably spill over to the next downbeat. Therefore, the "ps" in this case should be placed on the last quarter note, as indicated below. When, in turn, the tenors finish the phrase, the "ps" should coincide with the second quarter note, and so on.

MENDELSSOHN, "He, Watching Over Israel" from *Elijah*

Another important element to take into account when deciding on the placement of a final consonant is the rhythmic implication of that decision. If we go back to measure 5 of the Mendelssohn example above and consider the possibility that, with a virtuoso chorus, we could probably place the final "ps" on the last eighth note, the resulting strong rhythmic clash of two eighth notes against three eighth notes in the accompaniment would be distracting.

In the concluding portion of the same Mendelssohn chorus below, it is preferable to place the final "ps" on the downbeat of measure 78 rather than on the fourth beat of measure 77. Since the chord of D major is repeated throughout the final three measures, any placement other than the downbeat of measure 78 would interfere with the peaceful ending Mendelssohn sought.

In the example below, we have compared the several ways of placing the final consonant when it is followed by a rest. However, it is clear that placing the final "t" of "not" on the second quarter note would result in an excessively long rest for the voices. Placement of the final "t" of "not" on the second eighth note of the second beat would result in unwarranted rhythmic excitement. But placing the final "t" of "not" on the rest (beat 3) can be done gently, will not last more than the value of an eighth note, and will leave just the right amount of time for a breath in anticipation of the next phrase.

MENDELSSOHN, "He, Watching Over Israel" from *Elijah*

Aspirated, Vocalized, and Final Double Consonants

The final consonant sounds "f" (as in enough), "ch" (as in church), "ch" (as in the German word "hoch"), "k" (as in meek), "p" (as in "hope"), or "t" (as in night) are not difficult for the chorus to execute properly. A final "s" (as in "greatness"), however, will very often sound too loud and too long. If the chorus has a problem in pronouncing a shorter and softer final "s," an alternate solution is to have some of the singers in each section omit the final "s" completely. This might be necessary, since the final "s" is the only consonant which increases in volume and duration in direct relation to the number of singers in the chorus.

The only way to sing a voiced final consonant is to add a neutral vowel [ə] to the final consonant. (Thus, the final "d" of "Lord" is sung "duh"). Failure to do so will often result in the transformation of that consonant into its unvoiced counterpart: "b" will turn into "p," "d" into "t," and a hard "g" (as in "log") into "k" (as in "lock"). "Lord of Lords" will sound like "Lord of Lorts."

Final "m" and final "n" cause no ensemble problems. In some cases, however, when they occur on a long note, you might want to start them sooner, since they can be sustained to create a humming effect.

Beware of words that end with "ng" [ŋ]. The words "long" "song" and "gong" end, not with a hard "g," but with the sound of "ng" [ŋ], which can be treated in very much the same way as final "m" and final "n."

When a final consonant is preceded by another consonant, as in "sleeps" and "Lords," the conductor, in specifying the placement of the final consonant, must emphasize that it is, indeed, the final "s" in "sleeps" that should be executed on the final quarter note of a full measure, and not the final "ps."

Do not place a vocalized final consonant on the following rest if the chord has changed. Since the vocalized final consonant has a pitch, it will clash with the pitches of the new chord.

Starting on "Y," "S," and "Z" Softly and Slowly

When a composition starts softly and slowly on a consonantal "y" sound (see *Jesu dulcis memoria* below), the conductor may encounter ensemble problems despite the fact that he has given a good preparatory beat. The problems arise from the fact that some of the singers may start forming the consonantal "y" (tongue against upper palate) too early.

They should be instructed to breathe with the preparatory beat and to form the "y" only at the very last instant.

VICTORIA, *Jesu Dulcis Memoria*

Exactly the same technique should be applied when a work begins with a soft "s" or "z" sound.

Unimportant Words

Prepositions and other incidental words should be sung the way they are spoken. Do not succumb to the temptation of overworking unimportant words with diction devices, because the chorus will inevitably give these words greater emphasis than they deserve. Two specific caveats might be:

> Refrain from using special devices like adding [ə] to the final "d" in the word "and."
> Do not pronounce the final "th" of "with" when it is followed by a word that begins with a voiced "th": "with thine."

Original Language Versus Translation

The question of whether a piece of vocal music should be performed in its original language or in the language of the listeners is one that will always be discussed, argued, and never resolved.

The advantages of performing vocal music in the language in which the composer has conceived it are obvious. In addition to preserving the idiomatic quality that is unique to each language, one is also reproducing the exact language sounds that were in the composer's mind.

On the other hand, if the audience (for whom we perform the music) does not understand the original language, is it preferable to preserve the sound of the original language and sacrifice instant comprehension, or to translate the music into the audience's language and sacrifice the original sounds?

Some performers choose to sing everything in the original language and supply their audiences with printed translations of the text. My own conclusion (after trying almost all the available possibilities during the past thirty years) is: When the text of a vocal composition is abstract (as in the Ordinary Mass and the Requiem Masses, where one basic idea occupies each movement), always perform in the original language and supply the audience with a translation. Thus, J. S. Bach's *Mass in B Minor*, Mozart's *Requiem*, and other works of this character should be sung in the original Latin.

When, however, drama and action are involved and instant comprehension is crucial, a translated performance is preferable. Thus, works like J. S. Bach's *Passion According to St. Matthew*, Mozart's *Così fan tutte*, Honegger's *Jeanne d'Arc au bucher*, should be performed in the language of the audience.

Singing in Languages Other than English

If you have learned the principles of good diction in English, it should not be difficult to apply many of them to other languages. Study the correct sounds of the language from the tables that follow and learn the characteristic connections of the language in question. You will find that you are able to sing and rehearse a chorus in a language that you cannot speak fluently.

Key to Pronunciation in Latin

VOWELS

Symbol	English Sound	Classical	Ecclesiastical
à	*a*go	compàrō	same
ā	*fa*ther	imāgō	same
è	p*e*t	propèrō	same
ē	*la*te	lēnìs	same
ì	h*i*t	ìdem	same
ī	k*ee*n	amīcus	same
ò	*o*ften	mòdus	same
ō	h*o*pe	nōmen	same
ù	p*u*t	ùt	same
ū	r*u*de	ūtor	same

DIPHTHONGS

ae	b*y* } *la*te }	caecus	caecus
au	n*ow*	nauta	same
eì	gr*ey*	deìnde	same
eu	f*eu*d } n*eu*tro (Italian) }	Orpheus	euge
oe	*oi*l } *la*te }	coepit	coepit
ui	gl*uey*	cui	same
ui after "q"	w*ee*k	qui	same

CONSONANTS

b	same	same	same
c	*c*an } *ch*erry }	cīvis, cantō, actus	same except before e, i, ae, or ao: excelsis, civis, caelum
d,f	same	same	same
g	*g*o } *g*entle }	genus, gula, gallīna	same except before e or i: genus, regīna
h	same	same	same
j	*y*es	jungō, jam	same
k,l	same	same	same
m	same	final m not pronounced	same

Symbol	English Sound	Classical	Ecclesiastical
n,p	same	same	same
q	same	used only before consonantal u	same
r	trilled	same	same
s	*s*ing / do*z*en	miser, mors, salūs	same except between 2 vowels or when preceded by voiced consonant: miser, mors
t	same but unaspirated	same	same
u	*w*ine	same except when preceded by q, sometimes by s, sometimes by g and followed by a vowel: quia, suāvis (but suōrum) distinguō (but exigūus)	
v	*w*ine	vīvō	same
x	si*x* / e*x*haust	exactus, pax	same except in words beginning with ex and followed by a vowel: exaudi, exhālo
z	a*dz*e	zōna	same

CONSONANT GROUPS

Symbol	English Sound	Classical	Ecclesiastical
bs	a*ps*e / o*bs*ession / o*bs*erve	obsideō, urbs	obsideo / urbs
bt	ca*pt*ain / o*bt*ain	obtinēre	obtinere
cc	boo*kk*eeper / ca*tch*	ecce, occīdō, occludō	same except before e and i: ecce occīdō
ch	*ch*aotic	pulcher	same
gg	le*g g*uard / a*dj*ourn	agger, aggrėgō	same except before e or i: agger
gn	di*gn*ity / ca*ny*on	same	dignus

Symbol	English Sound	Classical	Ecclesiastical
ph	*top heavy* } *phoenix*	phōca	phōca
sc	*scope* } *shin*	sciō, scūtum	same except before e or i: ascendō, sciō
th	*take*	theātrum	same
ti	*patio* } *ritzy*	nātlō	same except when unaccented, followed by vowel and preceded by any letter except s, t, or x: nātio, pretium

International Phonetic Alphabet: Italian Pronunciation

The consonants b, d, f, h, k, l, m, n, p, r, s, t, v, w, and z have their usual values.

Symbol	English Sound	Approximate Italian Equivalent
[ɑ:]	*father*	p*a*dre
[æ]	m*a*n	—
[ai]	f*i*ne	m*ai*
[au]	cr*ow*d	l*au*dare
[e]	m*e*n	b*e*llo
[ei]	gr*a*te	c*e*na
[ə]	f*a*th*er*, graci*ou*s	—
[ə:]	s*ear*ch	—
[ɛə]	h*ai*r	m*e*ro
[i]	fin*i*sh	*i*mmenso
[i:]	st*ee*d	v*i*no
[iə]	st*ee*r	v*i*a
[o]	d*o*main	d*o*mani
[ou]	r*o*pe	s*o*le
[ɔ]	bl*o*ck	bl*o*cco
[ɔ:]	f*a*ll	—

Symbol	English Sound	Approximate Italian Equivalent
[ɔi]	j*oi*nt	p*oi*
[u]	p*u*dding	app*u*nto
[u:]	m*oo*n	l*u*na
[ju:]	sp*ue*	rif*iu*tare
[ʌ]	m*u*ch	—
[j]	*y*ellow	rif*i*utare
[dʒ]	Ju*dge*	*gi*udice
[g]	*g*a*g*	*g*allo
[ŋ]	ri*n*g	carli*n*ga
[ʃ]	*s*ure	*sci*acca
[tʃ]	*ch*ur*ch*	*c*entro
[ð]	bo*th*er	—
[θ]	*th*in	—
[ɹ]	sailo*r*	—
[ʒ]	vi*s*ion	—

International Phonetic Alphabet: German Pronunciation

VOWELS

Symbol	English Sound	German Equivalent
[æ]	m*a*n	h*ä*ngen (South German)
[a]		*A*ntwort, fl*a*ch
[a:]	h*a*lf, f*a*ther, h*a*rbor	*A*der, H*aa*r, J*ah*r
[ã]	ch*a*nce	Ch*a*nce
[ε]	v*e*ry, h*ea*d	*E*nte, b*e*sser
[ε:]	f*ai*ry	F*äh*re, K*ä*se
[ε̃]		Bass*i*n
[e:]		*Eh*re, T*ee*r, *E*kel
[ə]	p*e*rhaps, id*ea*, moth*er*	*E*hre, b*e*antworten
[ə:]	s*i*r, h*e*r, f*u*r, w*o*rd	
[i]	b*i*t, h*y*mn	*i*ch, n*i*sten
[i:]	b*e*, b*ea*t, s*ee*, f*ie*ld	*ih*re, L*ie*ve
[ɔ]	n*o*t, w*a*nt	R*o*ck
[ɔ:]	f*o*r, w*a*rd	
[ɔ̃]		B*o*nbon
[o]	m*o*lest, *o*bey	

Symbol	English Sound	German Equivalent
[oi]		Hose, Boot, Sohn
[ʌ]	but, son, flood	
[u]	foot, pull, could	Futter, Pult
[u:]	do, boot, soup	Mut, Kuh
[y]		Hütte, füllen
[y:]		Hüte, fühlen
[ø]		Hölle
[ø:]		Höhle
[ə]		Parfum

DIPHTHONGS

Symbol	English Sound	German Equivalent
[ai]	my, wife, high	mein, Mai
[aɪə]	fire, higher	Feier, Reihe
[au]	house, how	Haus
[auə]	hour	Bauer
[ɔɪ]	boy, noise	neu, Baüme
[ɔɪə]	royal	Feuer

CONSONANTS

The sounds represented by the symbols b, d, f, g, h, k, m, n, p, t are more or less identical in English and German

Symbol	English Sound	German Equivalent
[ç]		ich, nicht
[x]	loch (Scots)	Loch
[ŋ]	hanging, thing	Ring
[ŋk]	sink	sinken
[ŋg]	finger	jonglieren
[s]	see, scent, receive	das, dass, Wasser
[ʃ]	shoe, bush, sugar session	Schuh, Busch
[ts]	hats	trotz, Zaun, Nation
[tʃ]	chin, patch, mixture	Patsche
[θ]	thick path	
[ð]	that, father, paths	
[v]	van, vine, of, gravy	wann, Wein, ewig, Vase
[w]	well, doughy, persuade	
[j]	yes, battalion	ja
[z]	his, zone, faces	Sohn, Sonne, Reisen, Sense
[ʒ]	measure, garage	Journal, Garage

International Phonetic Alphabet: French Pronunciation

VOWELS

Symbol	English Sound	Approximate French Equivalent
[ɑ:]	father, task	gaz, pâte
[e]	neck, stead	thé, melodie
[ɛ]	very, head	réel, gel
[ɛ:]	fairy	bête, dentaire
[i]	finish, physic	difficile
[i:]	seat, beat, field	dire, finir
[ɔ]	block, not	coter, voler
[ɔ:]	shawl, tortoise	fort, porc
[o]	domain	côte, gros, tôt
[o:]		dôme, rôle
[u]	good, July	tout, tourner
[u:]	noon, tooth	bourre, tous
[y]		rue, salut
[y:]		littérature
[ø]		neveu, rocheux
[ø:]		ouvreuse
[œ]		feuilleton
[œ:]		faveur
[ə]	perhaps, cathedral	premier

CONSONANTS

The consonants b, d, f, k, l, m, n, p, r, s, t, v, and z have their usual values.

[j]	yellow, yes	rien
[g]	game	degager
[ŋ]		agneau, soigner
[ʃ]	shield, sugar	charme
[ʒ]	vision, measure	engager
[w]	well, wall	oui, ouate
[y]		huile

Legato and Non-Legato Languages

Latin, Italian, German, and French, together with English, are the languages most frequently encountered in vocal music. A very important principle to remember, however, is that Latin, Italian, and French are legato languages. Most of the word endings are connected to the beginnings of the words which follow: "Salve O Vergine Maria." German, by contrast, is a non-legato language. When a word begins with a vowel, a glottal attack is necessary to separate the words from each other: "Da / untem / im Tale leufts."

In Conclusion

In solving diction problems, one important principle should govern all our decisions: technique is not an end in itself, but a means of improving artistic expression.

Suggested Repertoire: English: Mendelssohn, *Elijah*
Latin: Kodály, *Missa brevis*
Italian: Verdi, "Va, pensiero" from *Nabucco*
German: Brahms, *Four Folksongs*
French: Debussy, *Trois Chansons*

Chapter Six

STARTING BETWEEN BEATS

Very frequently, a composition will not begin on the first, second, third, or fourth beat of the measure, but rather in the middle of a beat:

MENDELSSOHN, *The Lark*

ROUGET DE L'ISLE, *La Marseillaise*

When this occurs, there are several convenient rules of thumb the conductor can follow.

Starting Without an Extra Beat

If the music starts on a note whose duration is *less than half of one beat's value* (in $\frac{4}{4}$ or $\frac{3}{4}$, less than an eighth note, or less than a quarter in $\frac{4}{2}$ or $\frac{3}{2}$), ignore the fraction and conduct a preparatory beat which will serve the first full beat of the music. (See Exercises 30 through 33.)

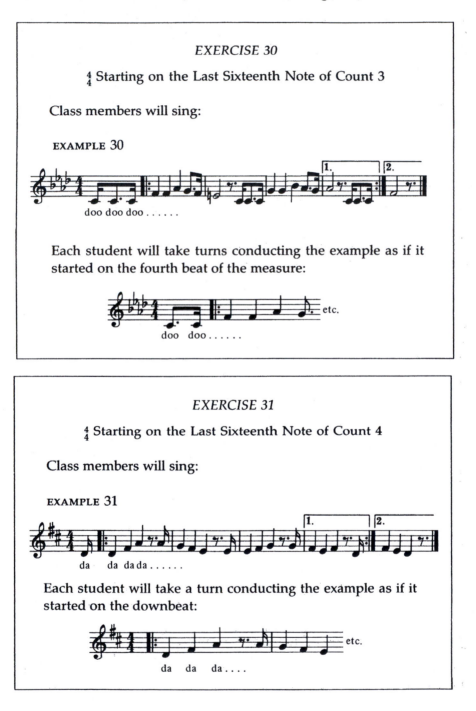

EXERCISE 30

$\frac{4}{4}$ Starting on the Last Sixteenth Note of Count 3

Class members will sing:

EXAMPLE 30

doo doo doo . . . . . .

Each student will take turns conducting the example as if it started on the fourth beat of the measure:

doo   doo . . . . . .

EXERCISE 31

$\frac{4}{4}$ Starting on the Last Sixteenth Note of Count 4

Class members will sing:

EXAMPLE 31

da   da da da . . . . . .

Each student will take a turn conducting the example as if it started on the downbeat:

da   da   da . . . .

EXERCISE 32

$\frac{3}{2}$ Starting on the Last Eighth Note of Count 1

Class members will sing:

EXAMPLE 32

da da da . . . . .

Each student will take a turn conducting the example as if it started on the second beat of the measure:

da   da   da . . . . . .

EXERCISE 33

$\frac{4}{2}$ Starting on the Last Eighth Note of Count 2

Class members will sing:

EXAMPLE 33

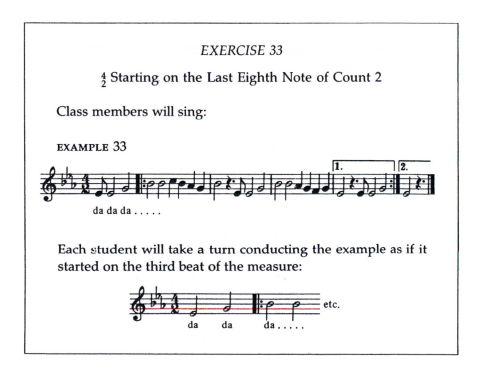

da da da . . . . .

Each student will take a turn conducting the example as if it started on the third beat of the measure:

da   da   da . . . . .

Starting With an Extra Beat

If the music commences on a fraction that is *half or more than half of the beat's value* (see example below), it is necessary to conduct an additional preparatory beat on the previous count. This additional beat must be a smooth *neutral beat*.

Neutral
Beat on Count 3

A *neutral beat* is necessary because a strong, bouncy beat on 3 will make it very difficult for even the best-trained choir to resist coming in *on* 4 or even earlier, rather than on the second sixteenth note of the fourth beat.

When conducting a neutral beat, avoid even the smallest bounce at its commencement (see conducting diagram for Exercise 34).

The *neutral beat* serves to indicate to the ensemble the expected length of each beat (i.e., it sets the tempo).

EXERCISE 34

$\frac{4}{4}$ + Dotted-Eighth-Note Upbeat

Class members take turns conducting the following pattern:

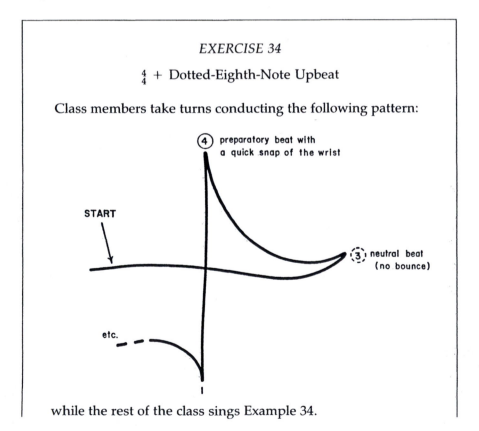

while the rest of the class sings Example 34.

Starting Between Beats

EXAMPLE 34

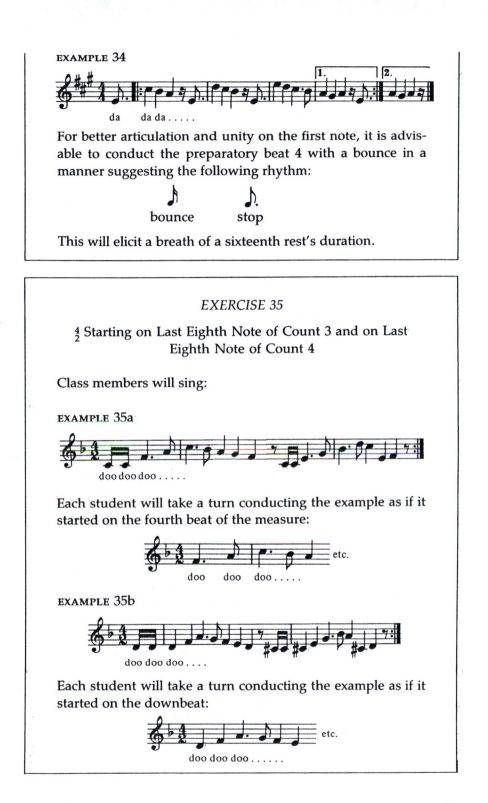

da   da da . . . . .

For better articulation and unity on the first note, it is advisable to conduct the preparatory beat 4 with a bounce in a manner suggesting the following rhythm:

bounce   stop

This will elicit a breath of a sixteenth rest's duration.

EXERCISE 35

$\frac{4}{2}$ Starting on Last Eighth Note of Count 3 and on Last Eighth Note of Count 4

Class members will sing:

EXAMPLE 35a

doo doo doo . . . . .

Each student will take a turn conducting the example as if it started on the fourth beat of the measure:

etc.

doo   doo   doo . . . . .

EXAMPLE 35b

doo doo doo . . . .

Each student will take a turn conducting the example as if it started on the downbeat:

etc.

doo doo doo . . . . . .

EXERCISE 36

$\frac{4}{2}$ Starting with Dotted Quarter Rest

Class members will sing:

EXAMPLE 36

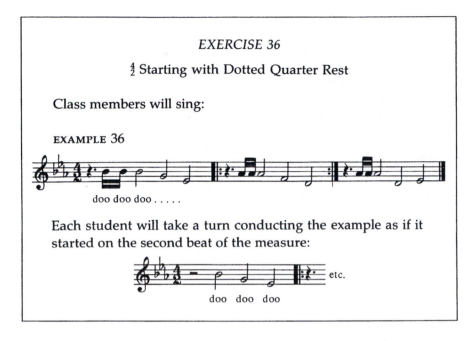

doo doo doo . . . . .

Each student will take a turn conducting the example as if it started on the second beat of the measure:

doo doo doo

EXERCISE 37

$\frac{4}{2}$ Starting on the Last Eighth Note of Count 2

Class members will sing:

EXAMPLE 37

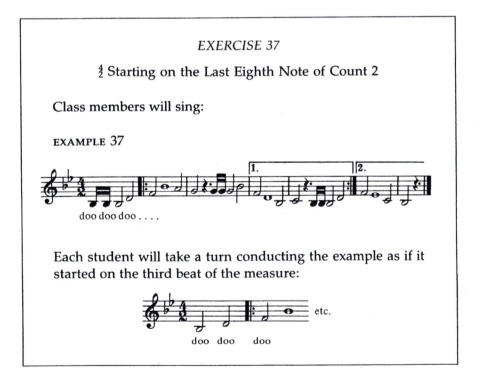

doo doo doo . . . .

Each student will take a turn conducting the example as if it started on the third beat of the measure:

doo doo   doo

Starting Between Beats

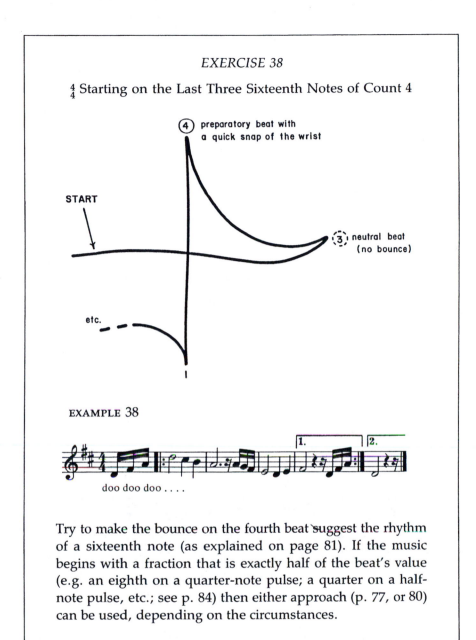

EXERCISE 38

$\frac{4}{4}$ Starting on the Last Three Sixteenth Notes of Count 4

④ preparatory beat with
a quick snap of the wrist

START

③ neutral beat
(no bounce)

etc.

EXAMPLE 38

doo doo doo . . . .

Try to make the bounce on the fourth beat suggest the rhythm of a sixteenth note (as explained on page 81). If the music begins with a fraction that is exactly half of the beat's value (e.g. an eighth on a quarter-note pulse; a quarter on a half-note pulse, etc.; see p. 84) then either approach (p. 77, or 80) can be used, depending on the circumstances.

EXERCISE 39

$\frac{3}{4}$ Starting on the Last Eighth Note of Count 3

Students take turns conducting Example 39 with a neutral beat on count two. Compare the results in different tempos.

EXAMPLE 39

da da da . . . .

EXERCISE 40

$\frac{4}{2}$ Starting on the Middle of the Second Beat)

Students take turns conducting Example 40 with a neutral beat on count one.

EXAMPLE 40

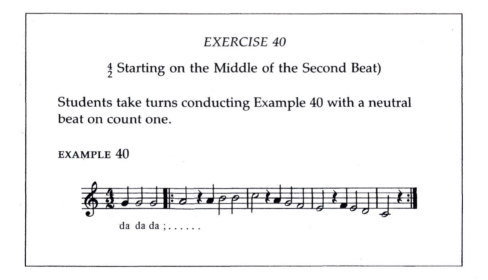

da da da ; . . . . . .

Suggested Repertoire: **Mendelssohn,** *The Lark*
Brahms, Fifth movement of the *German Requiem*
Bach, Versus IV from Cantata No. 4, *Christ lag in*
Todesbanden
Haydn, "Awake the Harp" from *The Creation*

EXERCISE 41

$\frac{2}{4}$ Starting on a Fraction of Count 2

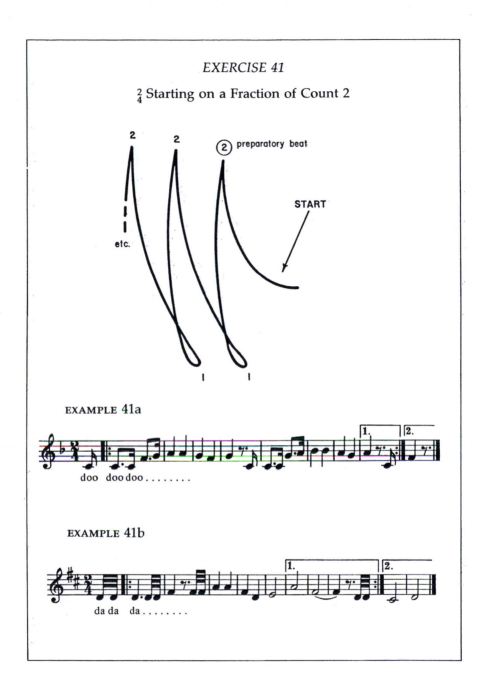

EXAMPLE 41a

doo doo doo........

EXAMPLE 41b

da da da........

EXERCISE 42

$\frac{2}{4}$ Starting on Second Eighth Note of Count 2

While class members sing Example 42, students take turns conducting, first using the diagram for Exercise 41 on p. 85, then using the diagram below. Compare the results by conducting each at a different tempo.

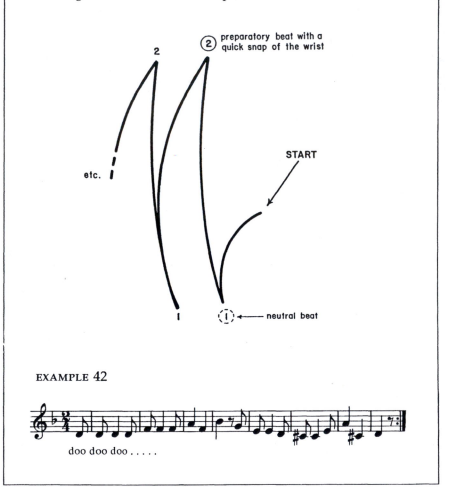

EXAMPLE 42

doo doo doo . . . . .

EXERCISE 43

$\frac{2}{4}$ Starting on Last Three Sixteenth Notes of Count 2

EXAMPLE 43

doo doo doo . . . . .

Suggested Repertoire: Handel, "The People That Walked in Darkness" from *Messiah*

Haydn, "The Heavens Are Telling" from *The Creation*

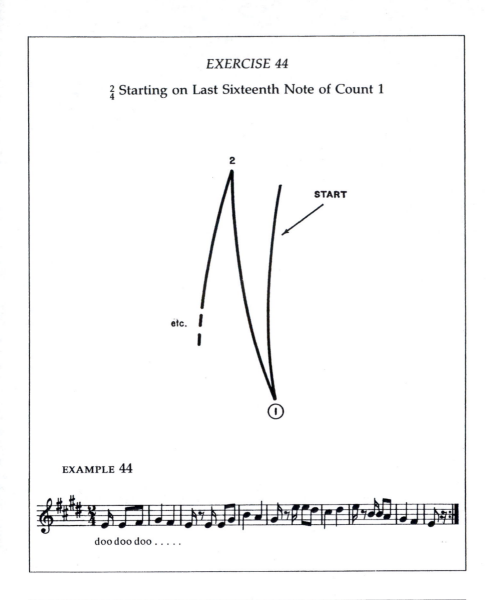

EXERCISE 44

$\frac{2}{4}$ Starting on Last Sixteenth Note of Count 1

2

START

etc.

①

EXAMPLE 44

doo doo doo . . . . .

EXERCISE 45

$\frac{2}{4}$ Starting on Second Eighth of Count 1

While class members sing Example 45, students take turns conducting it, first using the diagram in Exercise 44, then using the diagram on page 89. Compare the results obtained while conducting each of the diagrams at different speeds.

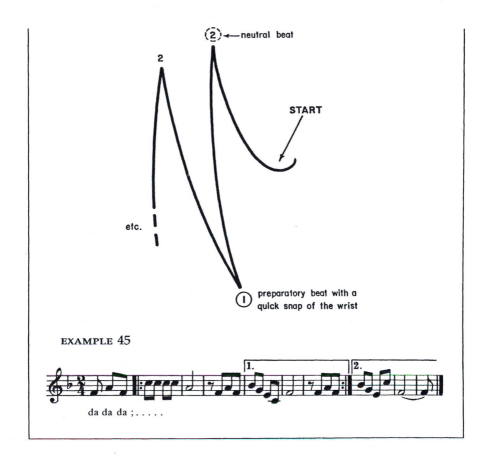

EXAMPLE 45

da da da ; . . . . .

EXERCISE 46

$\frac{2}{4}$ Starting with a Sixteenth Rest

Conduct Example 46 using diagram above.

EXAMPLE 46

doo doo doo . . . .

Suggested Repertoire: Schubert, Credo from *Mass No. 2 in G major*
Victoria, *Jesu dulcis, O vos omnes* and *Ave Maria*
Brahms, *In stille Nacht*
Verdi, *Ave Maria* from *Quatro pezzi sacri*

Chapter Seven

DISCIPLINE

"Why Are Choruses Always Behind the Conductor's Beat?"

Choruses seem to be capable of performing a remarkable feat: although they sing together, they are often a bit *behind* the conductor's beat. What is remarkable is that they stay together as they do this.

This phenomenon is caused by one (or more) of the following:

1. *The conductor's beat.* When you arrive at a beat sooner than the instant implied by the preceding beats, the chorus (and / or orchestra) will seem to be late. This can be remedied by making your beat more precise.

   One thing you should not do is "push ahead" to "make up for the delay." That is the kind of irregular beat that created the problem in the first place and will only aggravate it.

2. *The chorus sight-reading.* When a chorus is learning a new piece which taxes its sight-reading ability to the limit, a "let's wait for each other" attitude may prevail among some of the singers. The result is a consistent lagging behind the conductor's beat. This problem should disappear once the singers have all learned the music.

3. *Late start on syllables beginning with aspirated consonants.* When a syllable commences with an aspirated consonant, for example, "ein *Spott*" (J. S. Bach, Cantata No. 4) the chorus very often will start it with the conductor's beat. However, a syllable which starts with an aspirated consonant has no pitch until the following vowel is sung. Therefore, when those syllables are sung with orchestral accompaniment, the chorus always seems to be late—and it is!

   The remedy for this problem is quite simple: have your chorus execute the vowel sound of each syllable on the beat

90

to which it belongs, and *anticipate* the aspirated initial consonants.

This last example of chorus lateness most often manifests itself in
slow and sustained music. It is also the cause least frequently detected
by conductors, who comfort themselves with the thought that "Choruses are always late." But they are not! A truer statement is that choruses are often poorly trained.

To Memorize or Not to Memorize

Two anecdotes may serve to illustrate the pros and cons of the memori-
zation question:

When the late Italian maestro Arturo Toscanini was asked why he
conducted so often without a score, he is reported to have answered: "It
is better for a conductor to have the score in his head, rather than his
head in the score."

When the late German maestro Otto Klemperer (who was known
to have a phenomenal memory) was asked why he always conducted
with a score, his answer (after a short, thoughtful pause) was: "But I do
know how to read a score!"

Both stories point up some advantages and disadvantages that can
result from conducting with or without a score. It is clearly an advantage
to all concerned if the conductor does not have to have his head buried
in the score. However, if the conductor ever has to think "What comes
next?" or "I'll just continue beating time until I hear something familiar," then it is infinitely preferable to perform with a score.

Of course, it is entirely possible to develop your conducting technique with a score while still retaining a sense of continuity and overall
form. Therefore, we may conclude that it is advisable to conduct from
memory if it does not add extra tension to your performance.

I have personally found that the best way to *study* a score is to
memorize it.

Mannerisms

Conducting mannerisms include gestures, body motions, and instruc-
tional phrases which are repeated, not for specifically musical reasons,
but from habit or as a manifestation of nervous tension. At best, mannerisms are harmless; at worst, they are detrimental to the musical performance.

One of the most common mannerisms peculiar to choral conducting is the exaggerated mouthing of the text. Conductors guilty of this extraneous and misguided exercise in togetherness rationalize that "If I do not mouth the words for my chorus, they will not be able to sing," or "If I do not mouth the words, my chorus will never enunciate the text properly." Obviously, if the chorus needs to lip-read the text from the conductor's distant and distorted mouthing, they must be totally unfamiliar with the work, have not been properly rehearsed, and should not be performing it at that time.

Further, the conductor's grimaces produced by mouthing the text would prove a distraction from the appropriate conducting gestures. In short, the only dependency the conductor should foster is on the conducting patterns specifically designed for the work at hand.

Another common conducting mannerism is gesturing with both hands in mirror fashion. All conducting motions should be like precision tools in a craftman's hands. You pick up the hammer to drive a nail; you take the saw to cut wood; but you do not hold a hammer in each hand or saw all day just because it "feels good." Don't make any conducting motion merely because you enjoy it! Get rid of conducting motions that control you! The only motions essential for communicating with your ensemble are the conducting patterns.

Rehearsal mannerisms also diminish a conductor's effectiveness. For example, if you find yourself repeating the same instruction with the same words all through a rehearsal, you can be sure that you have slipped into a verbal mannerism and your instructions will fall on deaf ears, as a result.

"You must breathe before you sing a musical phrase" is a statement that contains an indispensable directive. However, the way to instill this good habit in your singers is not to repeat the statement *ad nauseam*. One does not have to have a Ph. D. in psychology to know that the more often you repeat a phrase the greater the chance that your listeners will "turn you off"completely and not hear you at all. Even if you have a burning desire to impart certain great truths to your chorus, remember: don't repeat, *paraphrase*.

The easiest way to spot any mannerism in oneself is to try to conduct without it. If you find yourself slipping back into it unconsciously, then it is a mannerism. A mannerism is a motion (or habit) that controls you, rather than being controlled by you.

The Unlimited Right to Speak

One of the most frequent causes of a conductor's downfall has been "too much talk." Do not abuse your unlimited right to speak. While members

Discipline

of the chorus and orchestra have to request permission to talk during rehearsal, your right to address the group any time you wish is rooted neither in an assumption of infallibility nor in hierarchy of position. It is merely the most efficient way to run a rehearsal.

The privilege is granted on the assumption that you are a good musician, you have done your homework (in score preparation), and you have an overall view as well as detailed knowledge of the work to be rehearsed. It is this total grasp of the work that the conductor is expected to communicate in order to make the performance a good one, and it is for this reason that—by gentleman's agreement, not by divine power—a conductor is given the unlimited right to speak. Use that right, don't abuse it.

Conducting a Professional Chorus

When conducting a professional chorus, you can and should expect a response similar to that of a professional orchestra. However the orchestra enjoys an advantage in that a certain amount of time and effort is usually devoted to the preparation of the string parts, into which bowings and other articulation marks have been inserted. Vocal scores are rarely marked with placement of final consonants, breath marks, and the like. Therefore, it would be wise for you to address yourself to this problem by careful study of the entire work and marking of the individual parts beforehand. If this is not possible, point out the places where special attention should be paid and have the singers mark the scores themselves.

Conducting Amateur Choruses

It is the common fallacy to think that, in order to conduct an amateur chorus successfully, you need to make bigger motions, mouth the words, or even abandon the usual conducting patterns in favor of "clearer" gestures. The fact is that what is good for the New York Philharmonic is good for the most amateur choirs.

The difference between an amateur and a professional choir is not in the conducting but in the training. We do not change our conducting technique to fit a group's lack of training. We rehearse and train that chorus to perform and respond to conducting like a professional one. Although it may take longer to achieve, the results should be similar. A performance of the Verdi *Requiem* sung by amateurs should differ from one sung by professionals only in tone color, but not in any other respect.

A parallel might be the comparison between a performance of the Beethoven Violin Concerto by a great violinist on a Stradivarius and a performance of the same concerto by the same violinist on a $100 violin. Both performances can be moving and meaningful, regardless of the difference in tone.

Therefore, when rehearsing an amateur chorus, use all your resources, knowledge, and rehearsal time to bring the group up to a professional level, but do not lower your expectations.

Stage Decorum

Suitable stage decorum, consisting of two considerations—how the chorus looks and how the chorus behaves—is essential for a satisfactory performance. The initial impression the audience receives is visually induced: how the chorus looks.

A unified dress code is very desirable. Choir robes are undoubtedly best, but there are some alternatives which can be adopted:

1. Gentlemen in black tie (white shirt, dark suit, black shoes, and black bow tie) and ladies in long or short black dresses or white blouses and black skirts.
2. Gentlemen in dark suits, dark long ties, and ladies in colorful dresses (avoiding black and white)

It is very important to train your chorus to behave properly on stage when they are not performing (during solo sections or when they are going on or off stage). When they are not singing, they should be sitting quietly with neither movement nor sound. Instruct the chorus beforehand on the need to find a comfortable but poised sitting position. Mention the inadvisability of crossing and uncrossing legs, fidgeting, or any untoward movement that will draw the audience attention to a chorister. Although it undoubtedly needs no mention, make note of the fact that whispering—even a desperate "Where are we?"—is strictly taboo.

Finally, the chorus deserves an explanation for this summary curtailment of their civil rights—and they should have one. Decorum and proper appearance of the performers allow the audience to settle down and listen to the music. Any unusual or inappropriate behavior on stage will distract your audience from the performance you have worked so hard to prepare.

Chapter Eight

THE PATTERN OF SIX

The Pattern of $\frac{6}{8}$

$\frac{6}{8}$ may be conducted in any one of three ways:

1. Using the pattern of *two:* In this case, each beat will be the equivalent of a dotted quarter note. All the principles learned in conducting 2 apply in this case, including the ones concerning the start on a fraction of either beat.

2. Using the pattern of *three:* In this case, each beat will be equivalent to a quarter note. All the principles learned in conducting 3 apply in this case, including the ones concerning the start on a fraction of each beat.

    The second option should be used only in the rare cases when a composer chose to notate the music in $\frac{6}{8}$ but should have used $\frac{3}{4}$ ($\frac{6}{4}$ but should have written $\frac{3}{2}$, etc.) See Francis Poulenc, "Hodie Christus Natus Est" from *Four Christmas Motets.*

3. The meter of six in *six* can be conducted in either of two internationally accepted patterns (see diagrams in Exercise 47). Of the two, the second pattern seems to be more frequently used. However, I have found the first pattern easier to follow. In any case, you should practice both patterns and be comfortable with both so that the choice of which to use will be based purely on musical considerations.

EXERCISE 47

$\frac{6}{8}$ in 6: two beat patterns

With the class standing in a circle, each student takes a turn conducting each of the beat patterns for $\frac{6}{8}$ in Six.

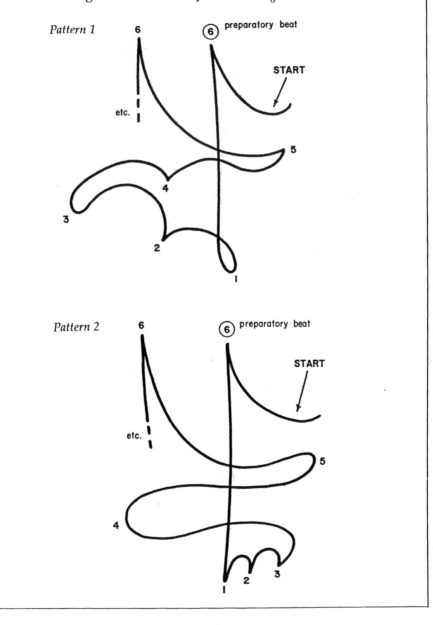

The most important principle to remember in starting on the various beats of 6 is: *Conduct a preparatory beat immediately preceding the count on which the music starts.*

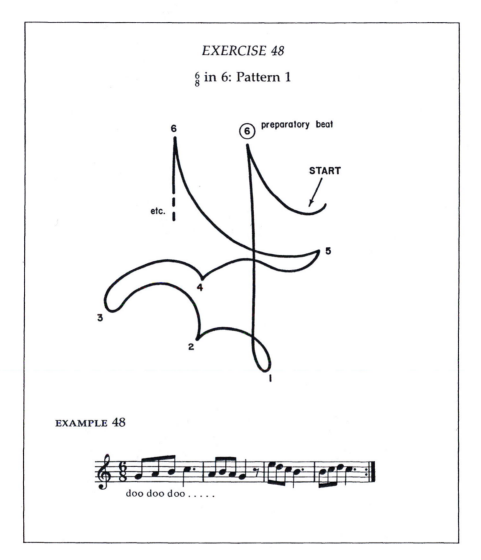

EXERCISE 48

⁶⁄₈ in 6: Pattern 1

EXAMPLE 48

doo doo doo . . . . .

EXERCISE 49

Pattern 1 in ⁶⁄₈ Starting on the Last Eighth Note of the Measure

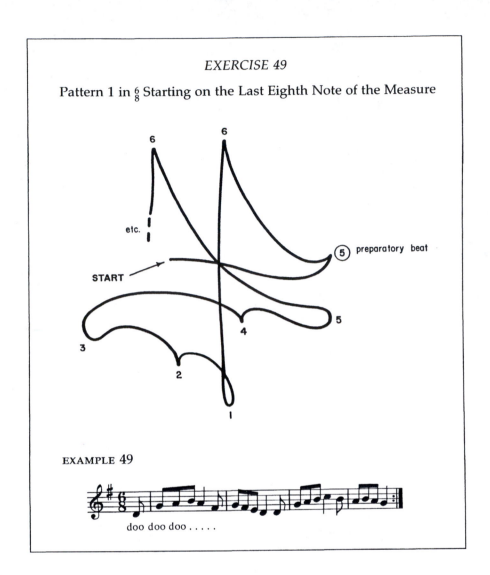

EXAMPLE 49

doo doo doo . . . . .

EXERCISE 50

Pattern 1 in ⁶⁄₈ starting on count 5

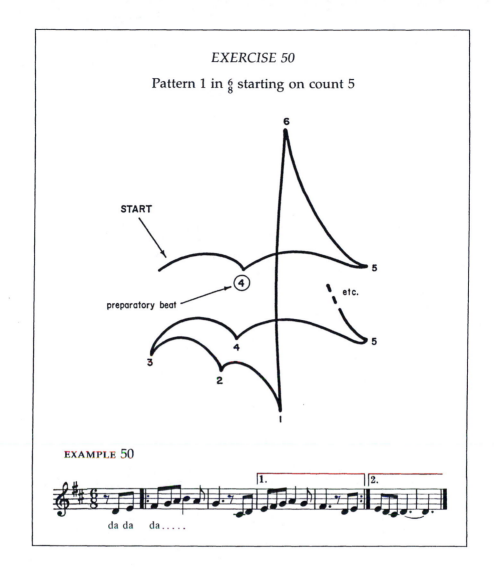

EXAMPLE 50

da da   da.....

Pattern 1 in ⁶⁄₈ Starting on Count 4

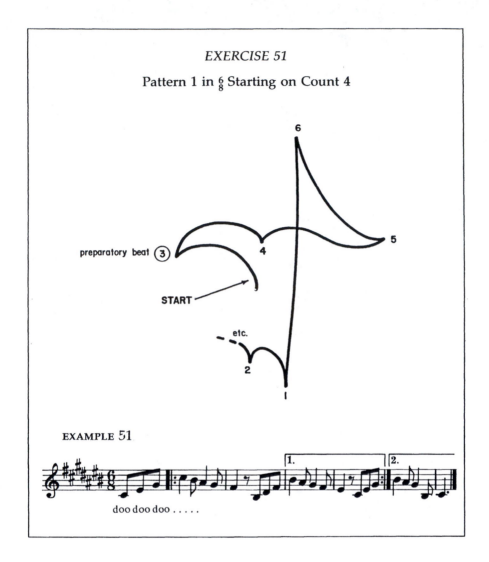

EXAMPLE 51

doo doo doo . . . . .

EXERCISE 52

Pattern 1 in ⁶⁄₈ Starting on Count 3

EXAMPLE 52

doo doo doo . . . .

EXERCISE 53

Pattern 1 in ⅜ Starting on Count 2

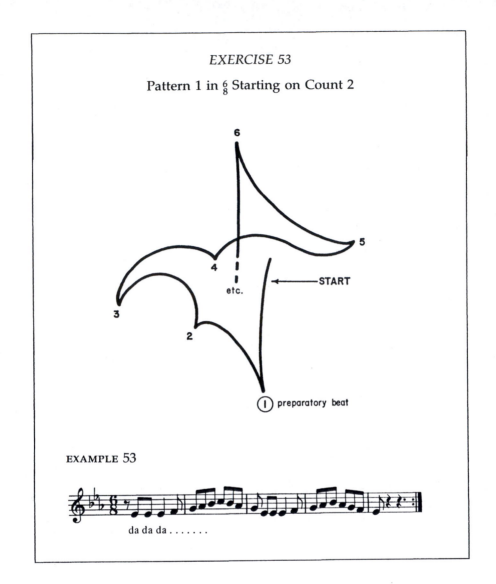

EXAMPLE 53

da da da . . . .

EXERCISE 54

Pattern 2 in $\frac{6}{8}$

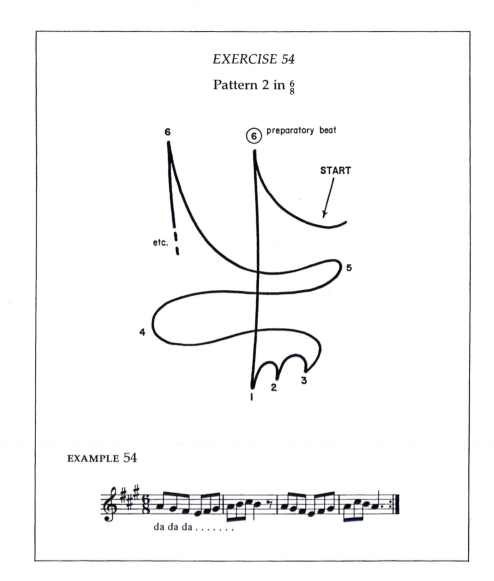

EXAMPLE 54

da da da . . . .

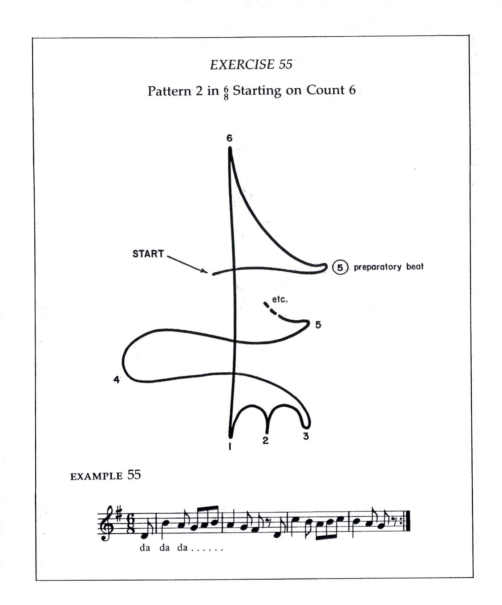

EXERCISE 55

Pattern 2 in $\frac{6}{8}$ Starting on Count 6

6

START

(5) preparatory beat

etc.

5

4

1   2   3

EXAMPLE 55

da da da......

EXERCISE 56

Pattern 2 in ⁶₈ Starting on Count 5

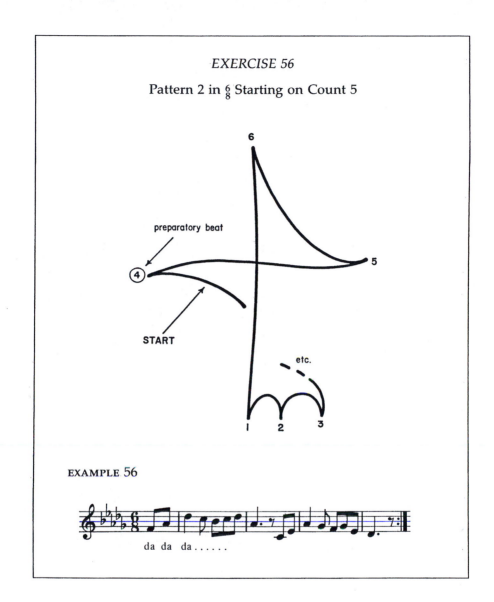

EXAMPLE 56

da da da......

EXERCISE 57

Pattern 2 in ⅚ Starting on Count 4

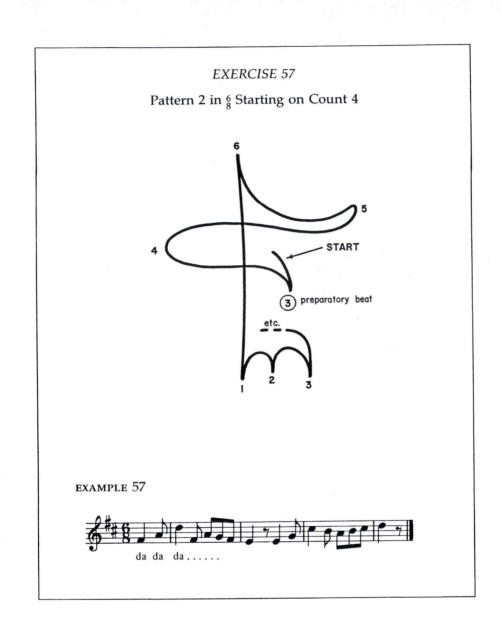

EXAMPLE 57

da da da......

Pattern of Six

EXERCISE 58

Pattern 2 in ⁶⁄₈ Starting on Count 3

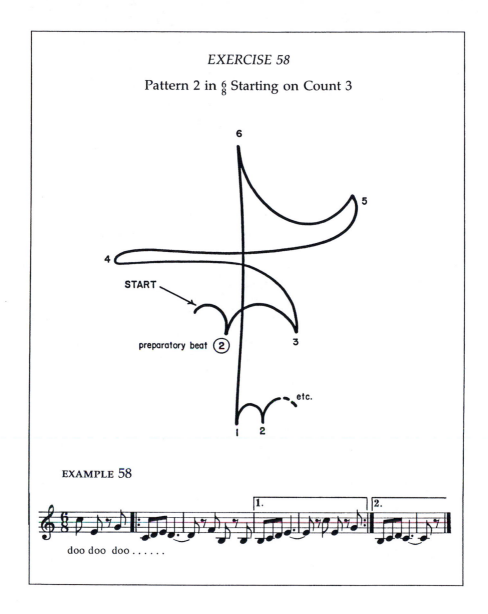

EXAMPLE 58

doo doo doo . . . . . .

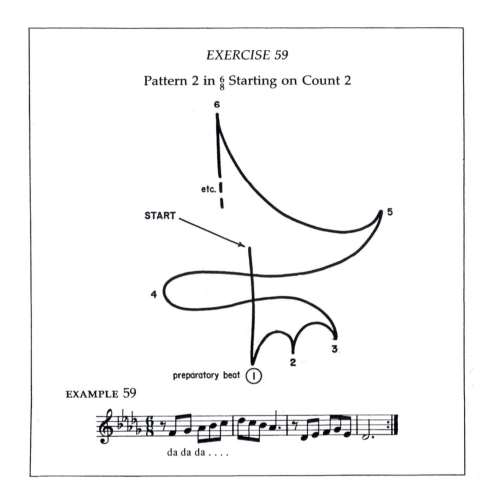

EXERCISE 59

Pattern 2 in 6/8 Starting on Count 2

EXAMPLE 59

da da da . . . .

The Patterns of 6/2, 6/4, 6/16, etc.

The conducting pattern used for all meters with a numerator of 6 are the same as those used for 6/8.

When 6/2, 6/4, and 6/16 are conducted in *six* each beat represents a half note, quarter note, and sixteenth note, respectively.

Suggested Repertoire: Schubert, Benedictus from *Mass in G major*
Weber, Agnus Dei from *Mass in G major*
Brahms, *Nanie*
Poulenc, *Hodie Christus Natus Est* from *Four Christmas Motets*

Chapter Nine

CHORUS WITH ACCOMPANIMENT

Chorus with Keyboard Accompaniment

Musicians who play orchestral instruments become accustomed to following a conductor's beat. However, since keyboard instruments are not used in the orchestra on a regular basis, most keyboard players never get this experience. It is important to remember this when programing a selection that requires keyboard accompaniment. Bear in mind also that when a keyboard instrument "goes off the beat" in either direction—by rushing or dragging—the chorus will tend to stay with the sound of the keyboard rather than the sight of the beat.

If you want a performance that has the spontaneity that results when a flexible chorus follows a conductor's beat, you must make sure that your keyboard player is following your beat. This can be accomplished by paying particular attention to your accompanist during rehearsals. Remember that it is difficult to follow a conductor while playing the piano; it is even more difficult from an organ, where both hands and feet are at work. Bear this in mind when preparing a performance.

Determine what relationship the keyboard has to the chorus at any specific moment. If the keyboard is playing an accompanying figure, it should remain in the background. If the keyboard part alternates between background and solo material, establish a balance that alternates between keyboard and chorus appropriately. When the keyboard has an extended solo section, give the accompanist free rein and do not conduct at all. When that solo section is accompanied by material of secondary importance, such as humming, consider the possibility of allowing your accompanist to take the lead with you following.

The balance between chorus and keyboard instruments should be determined in every case on the basis of the individual structure of the piece being performed.

The Choral Conductor and the Orchestra

A choral conductor who uses the internationally accepted conducting patterns successfully should have very little trouble when facing an orchestra for the first time. However, to be especially well prepared for the task of conducting an orchestra, the following steps should be taken:

1. Learn the music as thoroughly as possible. This applies to conducting choruses, too. (See Score Preparation, Chapter Two.)
2. Become as familiar as possible with what each of the orchestral instruments can and cannot do.
3. Familiarize yourself with the different articulations possible on string instruments, as well as with the effect various bowings will have on the musical phrase. Since the strings are the only orchestral section for which more than one player per part is required, the homogenous sound of the first violins, second violins, violas, cellos, and basses depends greatly on bowing and articulation. The way the conductor's knowledge of bowing affects the sound of the string choir is comparable to the way his knowledge of diction affects the sound of a vocal choir.

String techniques and the potential and range of orchestral instruments can and should be studied from one or more of the excellent orchestration textbooks now available to the serious conductor. However, learning to play each instrument at least a little and heeding the testimony of professionals on each instrument can prove most valuable to every conductor.

A sensitive choral conductor who has learned how to vary the preparatory beat in slow and soft music should have no difficulty discovering the subtle differences in cuing the string choir, the brass, or the woodwinds—even the subtle differences between cuing single-reed and double-reed instruments.

The Orchestra Conductor and the Chorus

An experienced orchestra conductor who uses the internationally accepted conducting patterns with his orchestra to good effect should have no trouble communicating his intentions to a well-prepared chorus. Do not succumb to the notion currently prevalent among some choral conductors that the chorus needs a "special" kind of conducting. If it does (and this will be discussed below), *the differences are not in the conducting patterns.*

To familiarize yourself with those aspects of choral conducting unique to it, I recommend that you scan the Table of Contents of this book for chapters that deal with unfamiliar subjects. In the following pages, I will point out some of the differences between choral and orchestral conducting as seen from the vantage point of the orchestra conductor.

Intonation

When, for example, the bassoonist in the orchestra plays an A♮ instead of an A♭, the conductor points out the mistake and that is usually all that is required. When a mistake like that occurs in a choral part or vocal solo, a similar corrective remark ("Measure 273, third quarter note is an A♭") should suffice. But if the mistake is due to the singer's inability to *hear* the note, it becomes the conductor's task to determine the cause of the difficulty and suggest a solution.

Diction

The orchestra conductor should be familiar with the manipulation of diction that is possible in the service of musical goals. For example, it might be sufficient to tell a clarinet player to mark the following rhythmic pattern

for a desired effect. However, a chorus singing

♪ ♩ ♩ ♩
All we like sheep

has to be reminded that the "w" must be quick and the "k" of "like" must be placed on an imaginary eighth note attached to the second beat, thus:

♪ ♩ ♫ ♩
All we li - ke shee- p
quick w

For a more detailed discussion of this subject, see Chapter Five on Diction.

Attack

An orchestra conductor sensitive to the different characteristics of the various instruments in the orchestra and the way they "speak" and react to the conductor's motions should have no difficulty with the attack sounds in choral music resulting from the use of different initial syllables.

How to Correct Wrong Notes

Finally, when conducting a chorus, the orchestra conductor must keep in mind a very important fact: **the voice is an automatic instrument;** that is, if the singer can hear the next note (in advance), he or she can sing it. The instrument closest to the voice in this respect is the French horn, for in addition to pressing the right valve, the French horn player must hear the note in advance if he or she is to have a fair chance of playing it correctly.

Obviously, any orchestral player who can hear the note to be played in advance will usually play with better intonation. But the danger of missing a note altogether because one cannot hear it ahead of time is characteristic of the voice and, to some extent, of the French horn and strings.

Suggested Repertoire: Schumann, *Zigeunerleben* (Gypsy's Life)
Mozart, *Coronation Mass*

Chapter Ten

THE PATTERN OF FIVE

The Pattern of $\frac{5}{4}$

The meter $\frac{5}{4}$ may be conducted in either of two ways:

Pattern 1: (2+3)

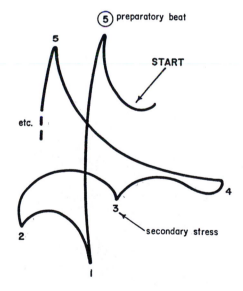

Pattern 1 should be used when the music to be conducted requires a secondary stress on the third beat.

Pattern 2: (3 + 2)

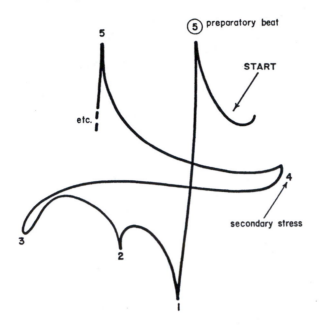

Pattern 2 should be used when the music requires a secondary stress on the fourth beat. When the music requires a change in the secondary stress, change your conducting pattern.

EXERCISE 60

The Pattern of $\frac{5}{4}$

A. All class members practice conducting $\frac{5}{4}$ with the secondary stress on the third beat (Pattern 1).
B. All class members practice conducting $\frac{5}{4}$ with the secondary stress on the fourth beat (Pattern 2).
C. All class members practice conducting $\frac{5}{4}$ alternating the two beat patterns.

The Pattern of Five

EXERCISE 61

Pattern 1 in $\frac{5}{4}$

With class members singing Example 61, each student takes a turn conducting Pattern 1 in $\frac{5}{4}$ (with the secondary stress on the third beat).

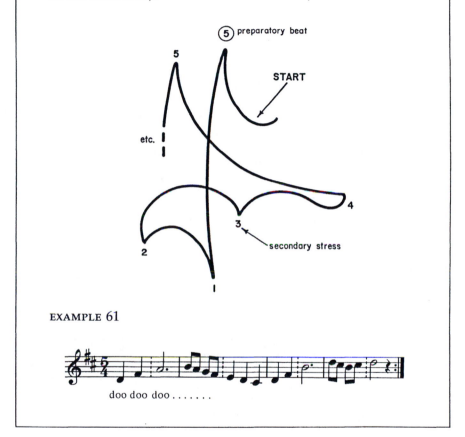

EXAMPLE 61

doo doo doo . . . .

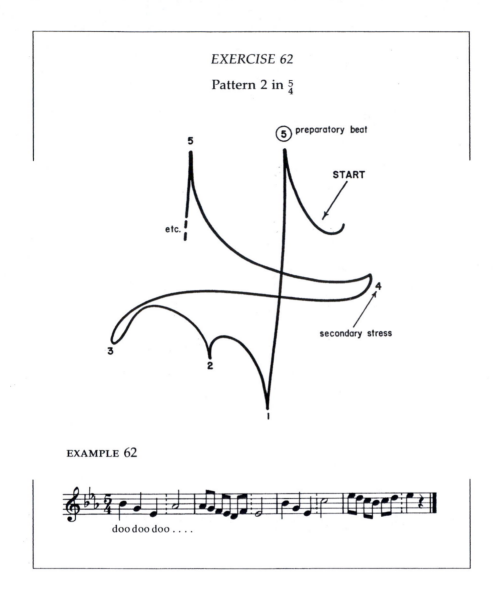

EXERCISE 62

Pattern 2 in $\frac{5}{4}$

EXAMPLE 62

doo doo doo . . . .

The Pattern of Five

EXERCISE 63

Pattern 1 in $\frac{5}{4}$ Starting on Count 5

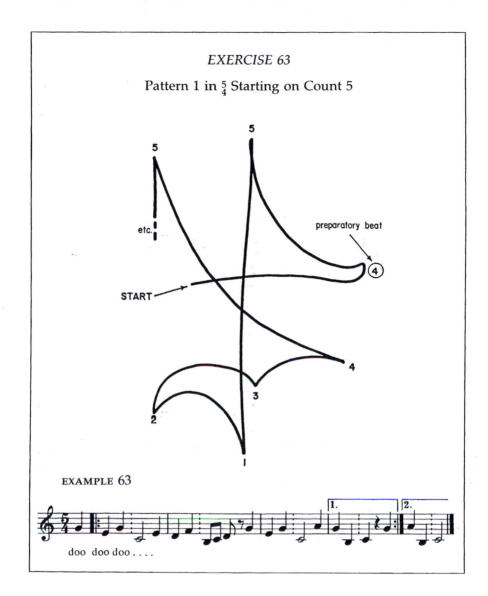

EXAMPLE 63

doo doo doo . . . .

EXERCISE 64

Pattern 2 in $\frac{5}{4}$ Starting on Count 5

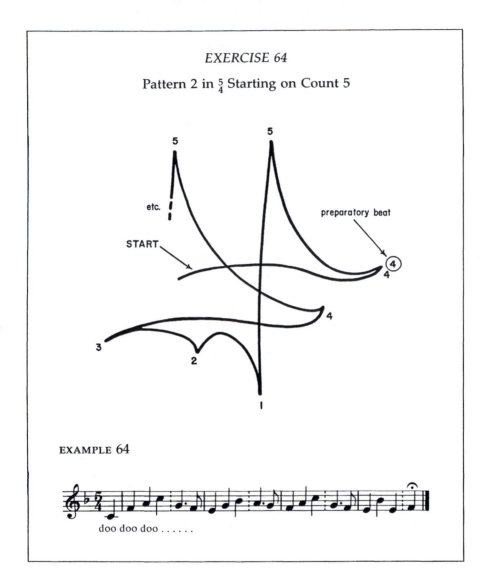

EXAMPLE 64

doo doo doo . . . . . .

EXERCISE 65

Pattern 1 in $\frac{5}{4}$ Starting on Count 4

EXAMPLE 65

doo doo   doo . . . .

Pattern 2 in ⅝ Starting on Count 4

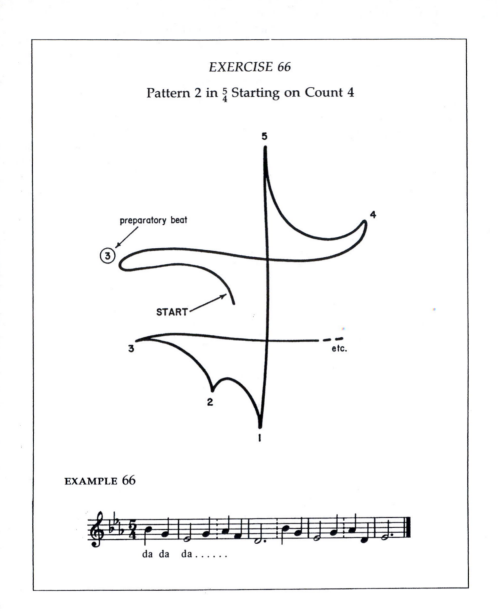

EXAMPLE 66

da da   da . . . . . .

EXERCISE 67

Pattern 1 in $\frac{5}{4}$ Starting on Count 3

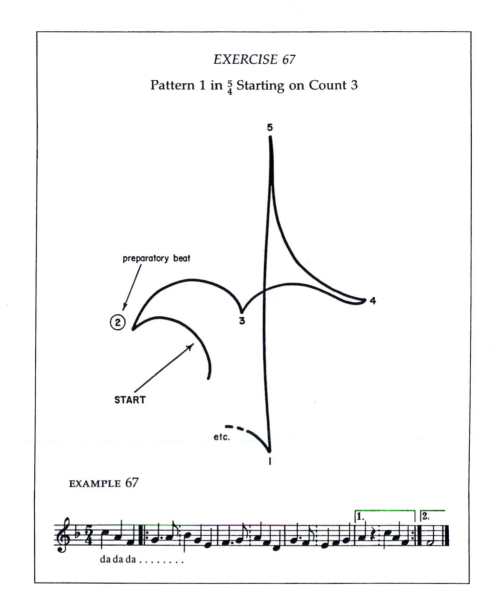

Pattern 2 in $\frac{5}{4}$ Starting on Count 3

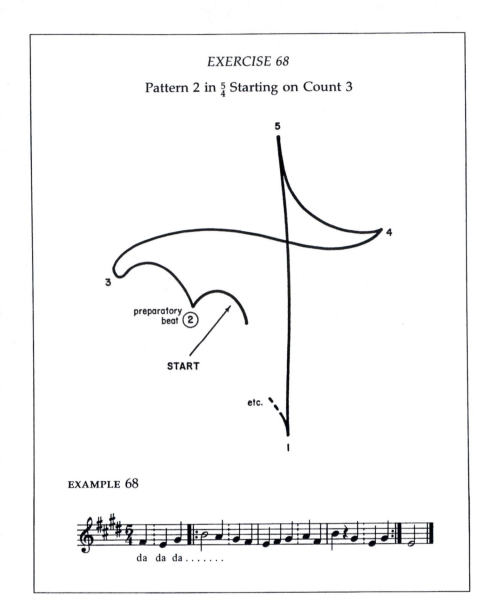

EXAMPLE 68

da da da.......

EXERCISE 69

Pattern 1 in ⅝ Starting on Count 2

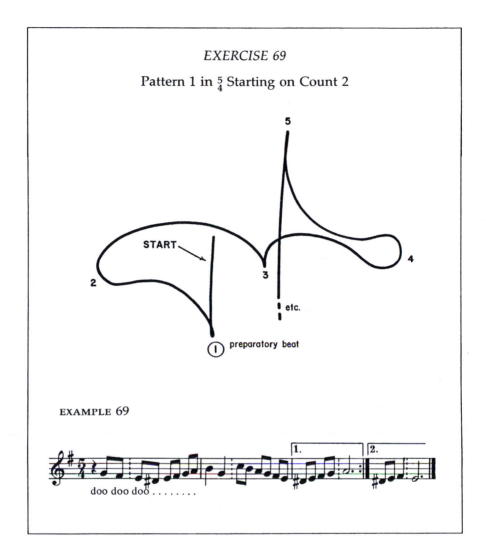

EXAMPLE 69

doo doo doo . . . .

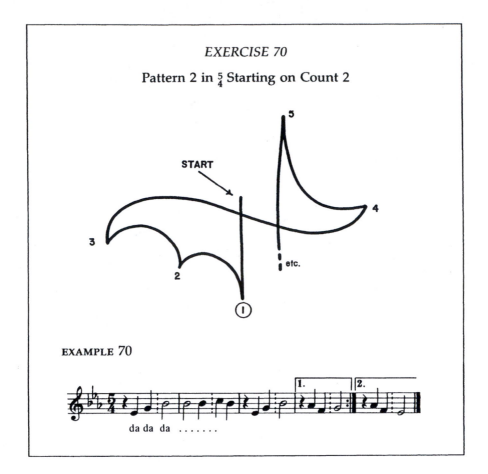

EXERCISE 70

Pattern 2 in $\frac{5}{4}$ Starting on Count 2

EXAMPLE 70

da da da . . . .

The Patterns of $\frac{5}{2}$, $\frac{5}{8}$, $\frac{5}{16}$ etc.

The conducting patterns used for all meters with a numerator of 5 is identical with the pattern used for $\frac{5}{4}$.

The Patterns of $\frac{5}{4}$, $\frac{5}{8}$, $\frac{5}{2}$ etc. in Two

For conducting a five meter in two, see Chapter Fourteen, *Meters with Unequal Beats*, p. 184.

Suggested Repertoire: Bloch, "Yimloch Adonoi" from *Sacred Service*
A. Kaplan, "Out of the Depths" from *Glorious*
Peter Mennin, *Crossing the Han River*

The Pattern of Five

Chapter Eleven

SUBDIVISION, THE PATTERNS OF 12 AND 9

Subdivision

When a composition has a time signature of $\frac{4}{4}$ and is to be performed at a very slow tempo, it is virtually impossible to control the ensemble with a regular pattern of four. In this and similar circumstances the solution is *subdivision*.

The Subdivision of $\frac{4}{4}$ in Eight

In Example 71 on p. 126, the time value of a quarter note is $\quarternote$ = ca. 40; thus the proportionate duration of an eighth note is ca. 80. The speed of the eighth note is closer to that of the human pulse and will be easier for the ensemble to follow.

Example 71 should therefore be conducted in a pattern of four wherein each beat is subdivided in two, as illustrated in the diagram on p. 126.

EXERCISE 71

Subdivision of $\frac{4}{4}$ in 8

Class members sing the example while students take turns conducting.*

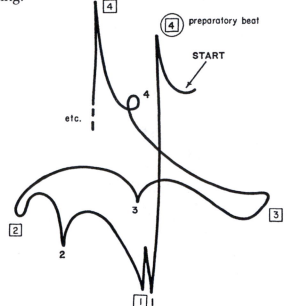

EXAMPLE 71: Bach, Kyrie from *B-Minor Mass*

* The subdivision of each beat is indicated by the boxed number.

Further Subdivisions

EXERCISE 72

Students take turns conducting each of the following diagrams:

A. Subdivision of $\frac{3}{4}$ in 6

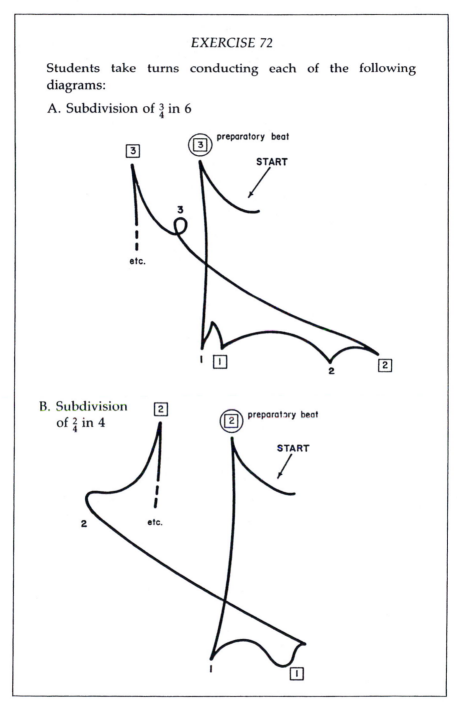

B. Subdivision of $\frac{2}{4}$ in 4

The conducting pattern for the subdivided meter of $\frac{4}{2}$ is identical to that of $\frac{4}{4}$ (See Exercise 71, p. 126).

The conducting pattern for the subdivided meter of $\frac{3}{2}$ is identical to that of $\frac{3}{4}$ (See Exercise 72A, p. 127).

The same approach is valid for subdividing $\frac{2}{2}$, C, and other similar meters.

The Patterns of $\frac{12}{8}$ and $\frac{9}{8}$: A Form of Subdivision

When the time value of the eighth note in a composition written in $\frac{12}{8}$ is closer to the human pulse rate than the value of the dotted quarter, the recommended conducting pattern is a form of the following subdivision:

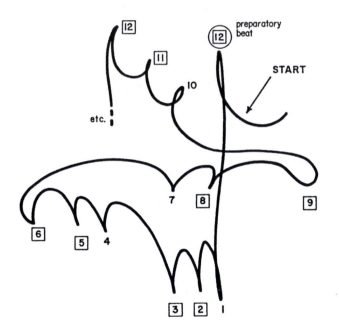

The conducting pattern for $\frac{9}{8}$ is as follows:

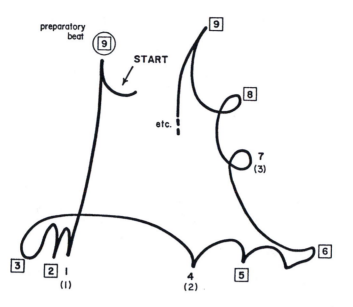

The Preparatory Beat in Subdivided Patterns

In order to determine where the preparatory beat should occur, all beats in a subdivision should be treated as equals: e.g., if the music starts on the *sixth* beat, the preparatory should occur on the *fifth* beat; if the music starts on the *ninth* beat, the preparatory should occur on the *eighth* beat, and so on.

Which Pattern to Use and When

When the time value of the eighth note in a composition written in $\frac{12}{8}$ is position (see examples below), choose a pattern that will make it possible to communicate the rhythmic requirements of the music in the simplest and most natural manner.

MOZART, *Ave Verum Corpus*

Is this in four or two? In the excerpt from Mozart's *Ave Verum Corpus*, the time signature ¢ reflects the fact that the music progresses harmonically in half notes. The indication *Adagio*, however, tells us that each half note should have an approximate duration of M.M. 42. But if this music were conducted in half notes, it would be very difficult to communicate the shadings and nuances of the quarter notes. Therefore, it should be conducted in four: $\frac{4}{4}$ or a subdivided $\frac{2}{2}$. In either case, the conductor should place the extra emphasis on beats one and three called for by the ¢ signature, as well as by the bass notes in the orchestra.

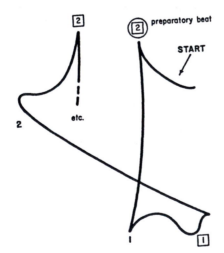

Subdivision: 12 and 9

SCHUBERT: Benedictus from *Mass in G Major*

Is this in six or two? In the Benedictus of Schubert's *Mass in G,* the decision whether to conduct in two or six will depend on how fast the conductor decides this movement should be performed. If the desired tempo is ♩. = ca. 60, then the pattern of two would be preferable. If, however, the desired tempo is ♪ = ca. 120, then the work should be conducted in six (since ♩. = 40 is too slow to control).

Personally, I prefer the latter.

MENDELSSOHN: "He, Watching Over Israel" from *Elijah*

Is this in four or two? If we compare the relative merits of conducting "He, watching over Israel" from Mendelssohn's oratorio *Elijah* in two or four, we will probably conclude that the pattern of two seems to serve the vocal line better. However, this will make it harder to maintain good ensemble in the strings' triplets. It would also be more difficult for the chorus to sing the rhythmic pattern of the main theme

$$\text{♩. ♪ | ♩. ♪ ♩} \quad |$$

accurately, without distorting it into

$$\text{♩ ♪³ ♪ | ♩ ♪³ ♪ ♩} \quad |$$

a rhythm that blends more comfortably into the triplet of the accompaniment.

I have therefore concluded that this selection must be conducted in *four*, with appropriate weight given to the first and third beats of each measure.

Summary

From the discussion of the preceding examples it should be evident that, in choosing an appropriate conducting pattern, you must first make some important musical decisions about the selection under consideration. Then you must weigh the pros and cons of the possible conducting patterns to determine which will best expedite those decisions.

If a change of tempo or musical texture occurs in the middle of a musical composition, you should not hesitate to change your conducting pattern. As an illustration of such an event, let us consider the excerpt from Bach's Cantata No. 4 on p. 133. It seems very clear that, at the double bar in the example above, Bach's indication of *alla breve* calls for the following conducting procedure: the pulse remains the same; the *alla breve* section is conducted in $\frac{2}{2}$ with the half note (♩) equal to the duration of the preceding quarter note (♩).

Suggested Repertoire: Bach, *Mass in B minor*
—————, Cantata No. 4, *Christ lag in Todesbanden*
A. Kaplan, *O My Son Absalom*
Mozart, *Requiem*
—————, *Ave Verum Corpus*
Schubert, *Mass in G major*
Vivaldi, *Gloria*

BACH: Versus I, Cantata No. 4, *Christ Lag in Todesbanden,* excerpt

Chapter Twelve

DYNAMICS

A conductor who has mastered the technique necessary to effect dynamic changes and tempo fluctuations is equipped with two of the most powerful tools for making music.

Sf (Sforzando)

You indicate *sforzando* (literally, forced or forcing; i.e., with a strong accent on a single note or chord) by an abrupt snap motion on the beat where the *sf* occurs.

EXERCISE 73

Sf (Sforzando)

With class members standing in a circle, each student takes a turn conducting the following diagram while the others sing the example.

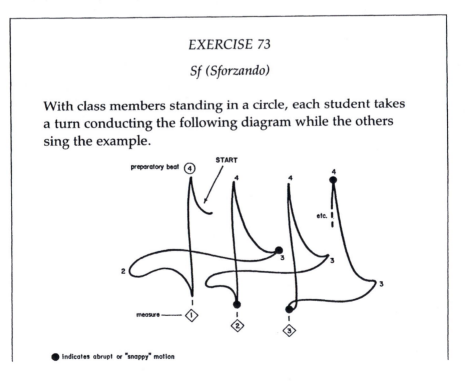

● indicates abrupt or "snappy" motion

EXAMPLE 73

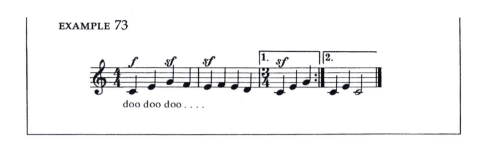

doo doo doo . . . .

Fortepiano

Fortepiano (fp) is indicated in much the same way that you indicate a *sforzando*. However, after conducting an abrupt beat where the *fp* occurs, do *not* bounce back to a full-size beat, but continue instead with a small motion.

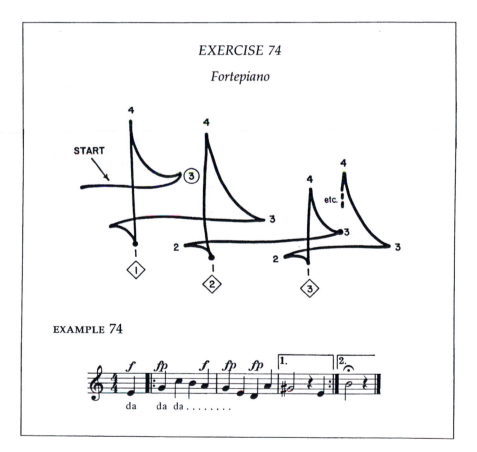

EXERCISE 74

Fortepiano

EXAMPLE 74

da   da da . . . .

Subito piano

To conduct a *subito piano* (*p sub.*) effectively, it is necessary to use a fairly large beat during the *forte* section and shift quickly to a small beat on the *piano subito*. Thus, if a *subito piano* occurs on count one, the conducting pattern should resemble the following:

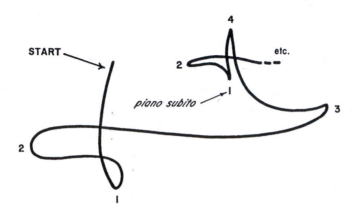

When the *subito piano* occurs on the fourth beat in $\frac{4}{4}$, the conducting pattern should be:

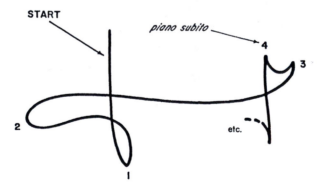

In some instances, a momentary cessation of motion resembling a brief hesitation is advisable just before the *subito piano*, as shown in the fol- lowing diagram:

Dynamics

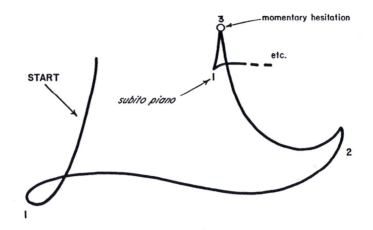

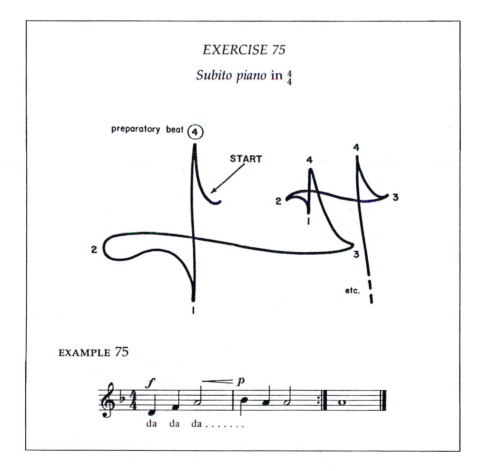

EXERCISE 75

Subito piano in $\frac{4}{4}$

EXAMPLE 75

da da da . . . .

EXERCISE 76

Subito Piano in ¾

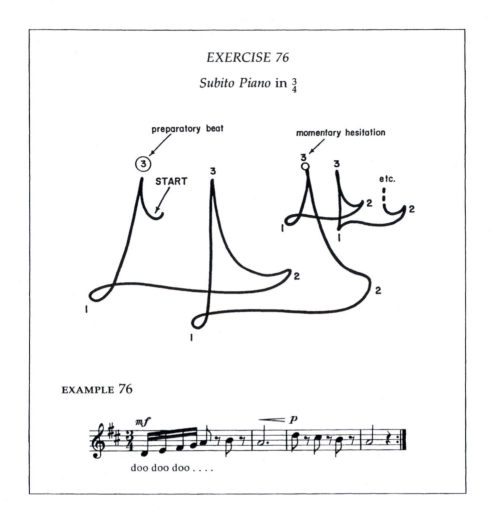

EXAMPLE 76

doo doo doo . . . .

EXERCISE 77

Crescendo and Subito Piano

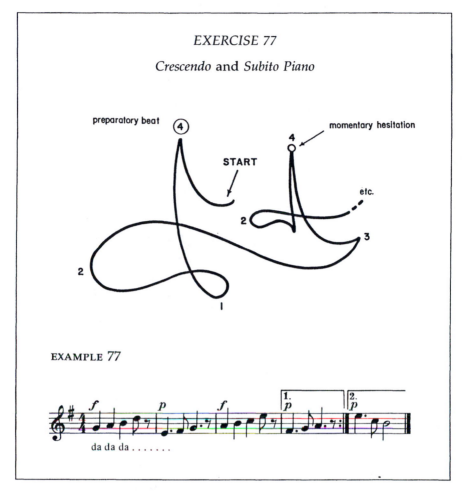

EXAMPLE 77

da da da . . . .

The left hand may be used to clarify the *subito piano* in the following manner: duplicate the movement of the right hand on count three with the left hand moving upward, palm facing you. Turn palm of left hand toward singers on count four in an abrupt motion and *freeze*. (See Exercise 78A on p. 140.)

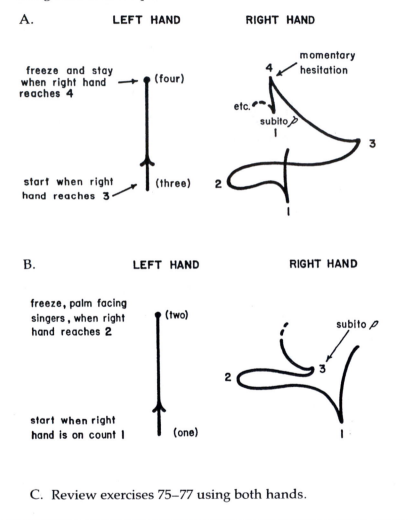

EXERCISE 78

Subito piano Using Both Hands

Class members conduct each of the following diagrams, using their own tempo.

A. LEFT HAND   RIGHT HAND

freeze and stay
when right hand → ● (four)
reaches **4**

momentary
4 ⟋ hesitation

etc. ●⁀

subito *p*

3

start when right
hand reaches **3** ↗ (three)   2

B. LEFT HAND   RIGHT HAND

freeze, palm facing
singers, when right ● (two)
hand reaches **2**

subito *p*

3

2

start when right
hand is on count **I**   (one)

I

C. Review exercises 75–77 using both hands.

The indication *subito piano* appears in music literature much more often than is realized. Every *piano* that follows an indication of louder dynamics (*mf, f,* etc.) without the benefit of a *diminuendo* to bridge the change in volume is, in effect, a *subito piano*. In some instances, a *piano* following a *forte* implies a diminuendo (but these are determinations that can only be made after thorough study of the composer's style and period).

Haydn, Beethoven, and Poulenc nearly always mean *subito piano* when they write a *piano* after louder dynamics without an intervening *diminuendo*. Haydn, the greatest master of *piano/forte* contrasts, rarely used *crescendos* and *diminuendos*, so when he left them out it usually meant he did not want them.

Subito forte

To conduct a *subito forte*, you must enlarge the beat preceding the count on which the *forte* appears. Since a steady tempo has to be maintained, the larger beat will be somewhat faster than its predecessor in order to cover the greater distance in the same amount of time.

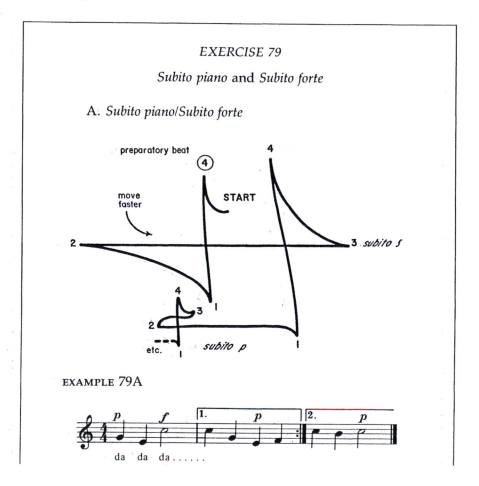

EXERCISE 79

Subito piano and *Subito forte*

A. *Subito piano/Subito forte*

EXAMPLE 79A

B. *Subito forte/Subito piano*

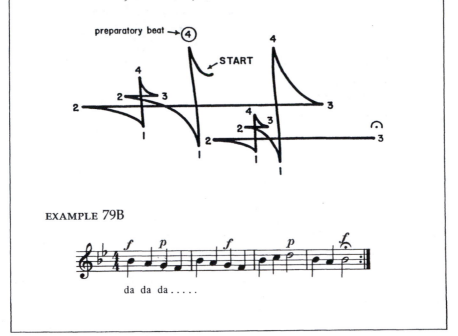

EXAMPLE 79B

da da da . . . . .

In the classroom, we can spotlight the technique for effecting sudden dynamic changes. However, as you gain in practical experience, you must develop a beat that will be a continuous chain of signals in which all dynamic changes as well as tempo fluctuations (including the most subtle ones) are communicated.

Suggested Repertoire: Schubert, *Mass in G major*
Beethoven, *Mass in C major*

Chapter Thirteen

TEMPO CHANGES, ARTICULATIONS, AND THE PATTERN OF ONE

Syncopation

In syncopation, there is a deliberate shift of the normal accent from a strong to a weak beat. There are two kinds of syncopation: the first, which has existed in art music for hundreds of years, may be termed *classical* syncopation. The second kind has its roots in American jazz, so we will call it *jazz syncopation.*

Classical Syncopation

In classical syncopation, when a weak part of the meter is combined with a strong part, a clash between the metrical and rhythmic stresses occurs.

For a cleanly executed classical syncopation, it is advisable to conduct the metrical stresses and let the rhythmic stresses clash against them; e.g. in the example above, you must give a strong downbeat on measure 2 and "think" a strong third beat in measure 3.

Jazz Syncopation

Although the notation of jazz syncopation may be identical to that of classical syncopation, the approach to its execution is completely different. If the rhythms of the example above were part of a jazz composition they would have to be read as if there was a hidden inner meter, such as:

In other words, a jazz syncopation shifts the *metrical* stress to correspond (rather than clash with) the *rhythmic* stress.

In the jazz syncopation illustrated in the rhythmic pattern above, beat 1 of measure 2 would have to be conducted lightly, as if it were an eighth note preparation for a ⅜ measure. The same principle applies to the third beat of measure 3. (Avoid a stress on the downbeat of measure 2 and the third beat of measure 3).

The following are four examples of syncopation from the literature:

BACH, KYRIE II from *B-Minor Mass*

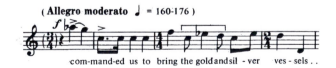

┌────┐ = classical syncopation

WALTON, *Belshazzar's Feast*

(Allegro moderato ♩ = 160-176)

·com-mand-ed us to bring the gold and sil - ver   ves - sels . .

┌────┐ = jazz syncopation. The entire $\frac{4}{4}$ measure is sung as an $\frac{8}{8}$ (3 + 3 + 2)

KODÁLY, *Missa Brevis*

⌐‾‾‾⌐ = classical syncopation

BERNSTEIN, RESPONSORY ALLELUIA from *Mass*

⌐‾‾‾⌐ = American jazz syncopation. Both measures should be sung as if written in $\frac{3}{8}$ starting with an eighth-note upbeat.

Close examination of jazz syncopation reveals its affinity with the irregular meters so prevalent in today's contemporary art music (See Chapter Fourteen).

EXERCISE 80

Classical Syncopation

With class members singing, first the Kyrie II from Bach's *B-minor Mass* (p. 144) and then the excerpt from the *Missa Bevis* of Kodály (p. 145), students take turns conducting the classical approach to syncopation. (If the class is too small, sing the top line in unison and octaves.)

EXERCISE 81

Jazz Syncopation

Follow the same procedure with the excerpts from Walton's *Belshazzar's Feast* (p. 144) and Bernstein's *Mass* (p. 145).

Sudden Changes in Tempo

To indicate tempo changes effectively, it is advisable to follow one of the following procedures:

1. *Slow to fast:* In order to change suddenly from a slow tempo to a faster one, the conductor, immediately upon arriving at the last beat of

the slow tempo, should use part of the duration remaining for a preparatory beat in the new tempo.

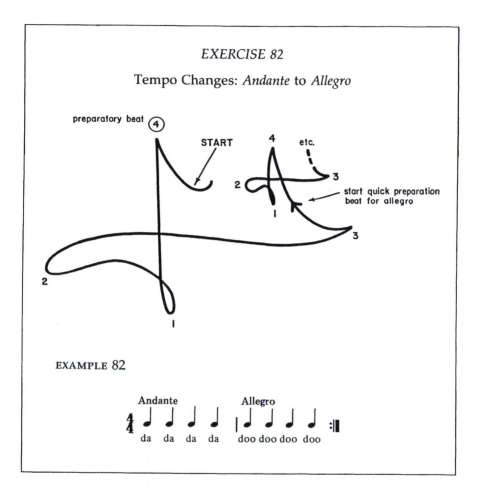

EXERCISE 82

Tempo Changes: *Andante* to *Allegro*

EXAMPLE 82

2. *Fast to slow:* There are two ways to change suddenly from a fast to a slower tempo. The one you choose should be determined by the musical result desired.

  a. Create a time delay between the fast and the slow tempos.

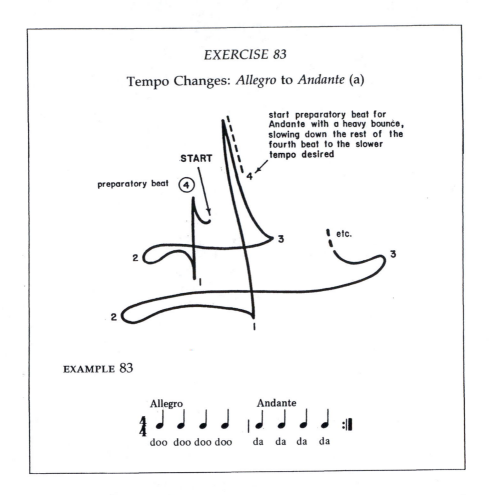

EXERCISE 83

Tempo Changes: *Allegro* to *Andante* (a)

start preparatory beat for Andante with a heavy bounce, slowing down the rest of the fourth beat to the slower tempo desired

START

preparatory beat ④

etc.

EXAMPLE 83

Allegro

Andante

$\frac{4}{4}$

doo doo doo doo   da   da   da   da

This approach will result in a longer fourth beat in the fast tempo and the effect of a time delay between the fast and slow sections.

b. Make a smooth transition between fast and slow tempos as shown below.

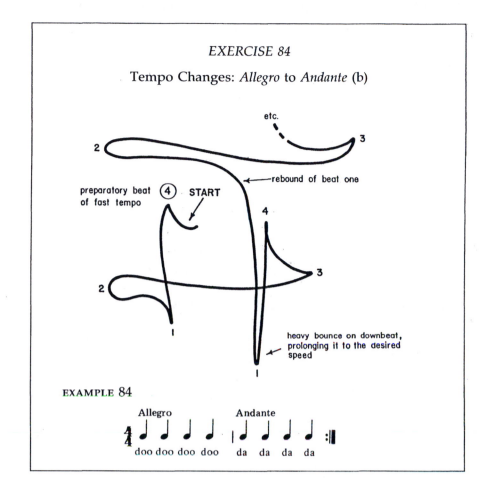

EXERCISE 84

Tempo Changes: *Allegro* to *Andante* (b)

etc.

2

3

rebound of beat one

preparatory beat (4) START
of fast tempo

4

2

3

I

heavy bounce on downbeat,
prolonging it to the desired
speed

I

EXAMPLE 84

Allegro   Andante

doo doo doo doo da da da da

Suggested Repertoire: Verdi, First movement of the *Requiem*
Schumann, *Zigeunerleben*

Simultaneous Staccato or Marcato and Legato

When there is a *marcato* pattern in one layer of a composition and a *legato*
texture in another, the right hand should indicate the former rhythmical
pattern regardless of the relative importance of the two contrasting tex-
tures.

The reason for this rule is that unified *legato* singing or playing is
perfectly possible against a rhythmic conducting pattern; however, it is
very difficult if not impossible for a group of voices or instruments to
maintain a rhythmic pattern while you beat a *legato* pattern, especially
in a slow tempo.

Furthermore, the rhythmic beat may be indicated with movements of the right hand from the wrist while a *legato* is maintained with whole-arm movements.

EXERCISE 85

Conducting *Marcato* and *Legato* Simultaneously

Class members sing the example below; students take turns conducting using a pattern that accommodates the line in the male voices. Use the left hand to indicate phrasing of the women's line.

EXAMPLE 85

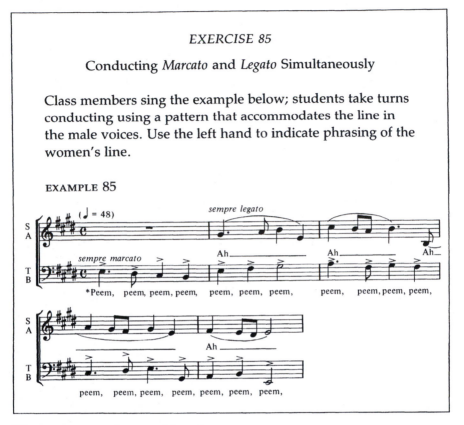

There are exceptions to this rule:

1. When a solo voice or instrument has the rhythmic pattern.
2. When the tempo of the music is fast enough, it is possible to sing a *staccato* figure against a *legato* beat.

EXERCISE 86

Conducting *Marcato* and *Legato* Simultaneously

Conduct Example 85 at a speed of ♩ = ca. 120, using a *legato* beat and concentrating on the women's part.

---

*Close mouth as quickly as possible at the humming sound of "m" on each "peem" to achieve an effect resembling an orchestral pizzicato.

Conducting in One

It is sometimes necessary to conduct a whole measure in one beat, as in the following two examples:

BEETHOVEN, *Symphony No. 5*, first movement

VAUGHAN WILLIAMS, *Wassail Song*

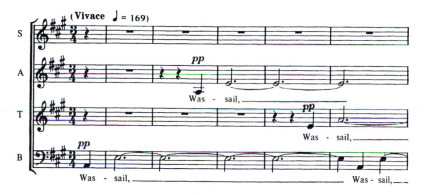

In both cases, the speed of the quarter note is so rapid that any attempt to indicate it with a conducting motion will either prove impossible or confuse the performers. In the Beethoven excerpt, we conduct a half note at a speed of ♩ = ca. 108, rather than ♩ = ca. 216.

In the *Wassail Song* of Vaughan Williams, we conduct one beat per measure at a speed of ♩. = ca. 56, rather than three beats per measure at a speed which would have to be ♩ = ca. 168.

Conducting in one is the ultimate test of a conductor's technique. In all other conducting patterns, an ensemble can recover after misunderstanding the beat by simply referring to the conducting pattern itself. However, when a piece of music is conducted in one, all the beats look alike, with each beat serving as a preparatory for the next measure.

Conducting in One

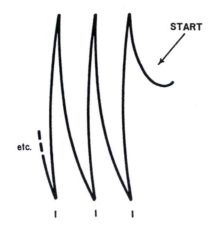

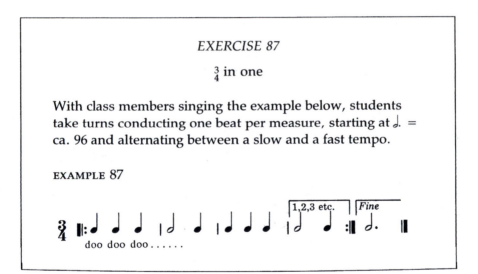

Very often in a composition in $\frac{3}{4}$ (or $\frac{3}{8}$) to be conducted in one, the
measures are actually metrically grouped into larger segments consist-
ing of two, three, or four measures. Beethoven does this frequently in
the scherzos of his symphonies and indicates the groupings and changes
in groupings with the words "*a tre battute,*" "*a quattro battute,*" and the
like (see example on facing page.) Even when the groupings of fast measures into larger metrical segments are not specifically indicated, these
groupings will inevitably manifest themselves. Thus, in the example from
Bach's *St. Matthew Passion* on p. 153, excitement mounts as the groups
of metrical measures get smaller.

Tempo Changes

BEETHOVEN, *Symphony No. 9 in D Major*, second movement (piano reduction)

BACH, "Sindblitze" from *St. Matthew Passion* (piano reduction)

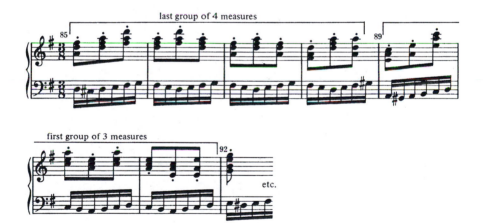

When a group of measures conducted in one forms a larger metrical entity (e.g. four bars of $\frac{4}{4}$ equals one large measure of $\frac{4}{1}$), the conducting pattern should reflect this by having a large *one* on the fourth measure of each four-measure group in preparation for the "downbeat measure" or the heavier one on the first measure of each four-measure group to represent the additional weight of a downbeat measure.

If we take another look at Example 87 (p. 152) with this in mind, we will see the pattern represented in the Bach excerpt above.

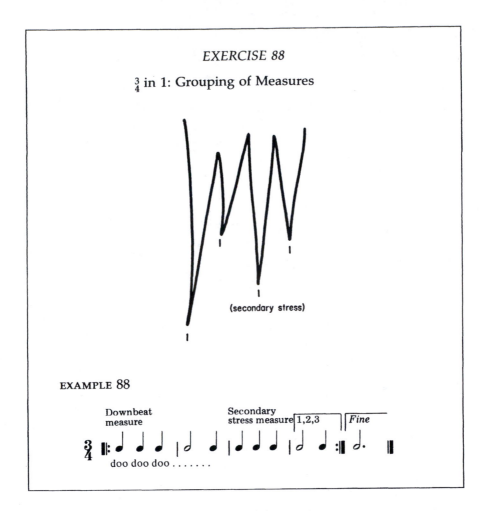

EXERCISE 88

¾ in 1: Grouping of Measures

(secondary stress)

EXAMPLE 88

Downbeat measure

Secondary stress measure

1,2,3

Fine

doo doo doo . . . .

Suggested Repertoire: Bach: No. 33 from *St. Matthew Passion*
German Carol, *In dulci jubilo* (Arr. A. Kaplan)
Vaughan Williams, *Wassail Song* from *Five English Folksongs*

Tempo Changes

Chapter Fourteen

METERS WITH UNEQUAL BEATS

Conducting Contemporary Meters

In this chapter we will deal with meters which have gained currency primarily during the twentieth century. Contemporary meters differ from traditional ones only in one respect: they require conducting beats which are usually of different durations.

When a $\frac{7}{8}$ meter is marked $\dotted{\quarter} = $ ca. 88, as in the example below, it is obviously impractical to try to conduct eighth notes at a speed of $\eighth = $ ca. 264.

A. KAPLAN, *Praise Ye*

*(3 + 2 + 2)

Therefore, each measure is divided into groups of two or three eighth notes, each group to be conducted with one beat. Since there are three such groups in the excerpt above, the regular pattern of three is used. However, since the first beat of each measure contains three eighth notes while the second and third beats have only two, the most practical pattern is a triple one, in which the downbeat bounce has a duration of $\frac{3}{8}$, while the second and third beats last $\frac{2}{8}$ each (see the diagram below).

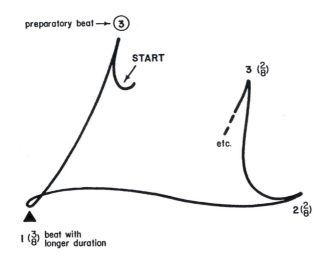

BERNSTEIN, *Chichester Psalms*, mm. 11–15

Meters with Unequal Beats

In the example on p. 156 from Leonard Bernstein's *Chichester Psalms*, the metronome marking is ♩ = ca. 120. To conduct in quarter notes, one would have to beat at the incredible speed of ♩ = ca. 240. Therefore, as in the preceding example, we divide each measure of the Bernstein into groups of two and three quarter notes and use beats with durations of $\frac{3}{4}$ and $\frac{2}{4}$ as implied by the music.

In the Bernstein example, we would use the pattern of three, with beats one and two each lasting $\frac{2}{4}$ and the third beat lasting $\frac{3}{4}$ as in the following:

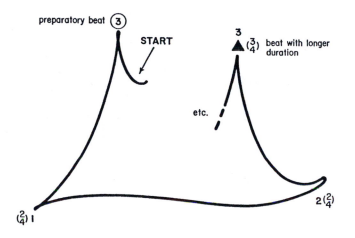

Conducting the Preparatory Beat

Since the beats in a pattern of contemporary meters differ in duration, a question inevitably arises concerning the duration of the preparatory beat. There are three ways to conduct a preparatory beat in contemporary meters, as will be seen from a close analysis of the excerpt on p. 158. We could begin with a preparatory beat having a duration of $\frac{3}{8}$, $\frac{2}{8}$, or $\frac{1}{8}$. In the preparation lasting $\frac{3}{8}$, we would use the second beat of the $\frac{5}{8}$ as preparation. In the $\frac{2}{8}$ preparation, we use a preparatory beat with a duration equal to that of the first group to be sung by the chorus. In the $\frac{1}{8}$ preparation, we indicate (preferably with a wrist movement) the duration of an eighth note, and as the music starts, we conduct the appropriate pattern of *two*, which is 2 + 3.

Whichever preparatory beat is chosen, it is essential that the ensemble be advised as to the duration of the preparatory beat in a contemporary meter.

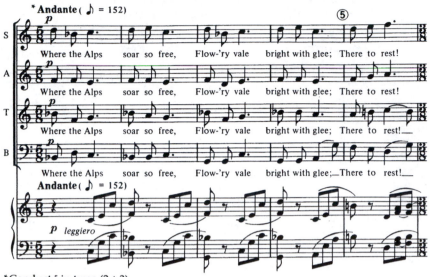

*Conduct $\frac{5}{8}$ in twos (2+3)

Conducting $\frac{7}{8}$ in Three

The meter $\frac{7}{8}$ (in a fast tempo) should be conducted in a pattern of three, with one of the three beats having a longer duration than the other two. The sequence of long and short beats is determined by the music to be conducted.

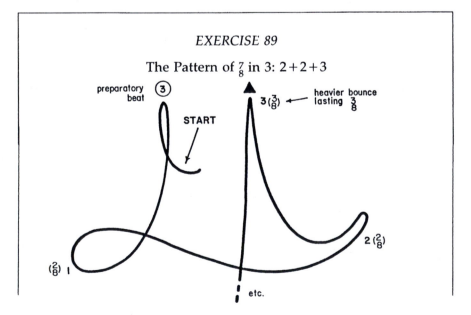

EXERCISE 89

The Pattern of $\frac{7}{8}$ in 3: 2+2+3

Meters with Unequal Beats

EXAMPLE 89

doo doo doo . . . . . .

EXERCISE 90

The Pattern of $\frac{7}{8}$ in 3: 3+2+2

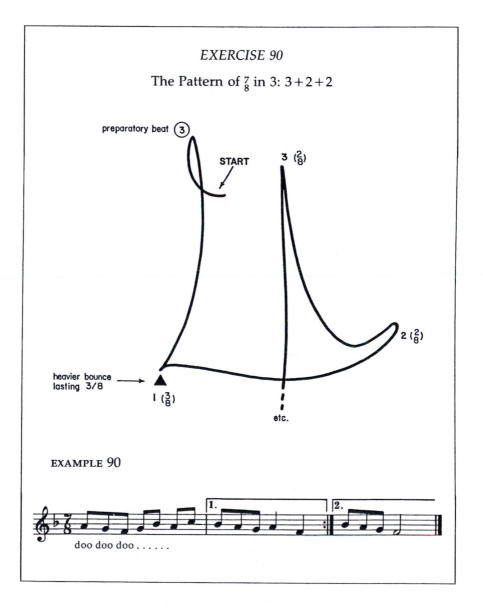

preparatory beat ③

START

3 ($\frac{2}{8}$)

2 ($\frac{2}{8}$)

heavier bounce lasting 3/8

I ($\frac{3}{8}$)

etc.

EXAMPLE 90

doo doo doo . . . . . .

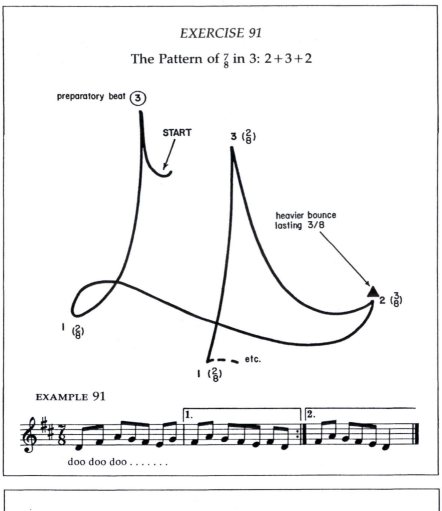

EXERCISE 91

The Pattern of $\frac{7}{8}$ in 3: 2+3+2

preparatory beat ③

START

3 ($\frac{2}{8}$)

heavier bounce
lasting 3/8

2 ($\frac{3}{8}$)

I ($\frac{2}{8}$)

etc.

I ($\frac{2}{8}$)

EXAMPLE 91

doo doo doo . . . .

EXERCISE 92

The Pattern of $\frac{7}{8}$ in 3, Combining Exercises 89, 90, and 91

Class members sing the example below, while students take turns conducting it with the diagrams provided in Exercises 89, 90, and 91 successively.

EXAMPLE 92

doo doo doo . . . . .

Conducting ⅜ in Three

The meter ⅜ (in a fast tempo) should be conducted in a pattern of three, with one short beat of ²⁄₈ and two longer beats of ³⁄₈. The precise sequence of long and short beats is determined by the music.

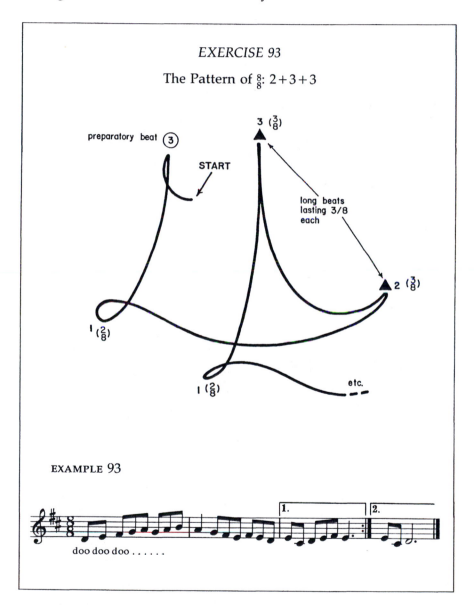

EXERCISE 93

The Pattern of ⅜: 2+3+3

EXAMPLE 93

doo doo doo ......

EXERCISE 94

The Pattern of $\frac{8}{8}$: 3+2+3

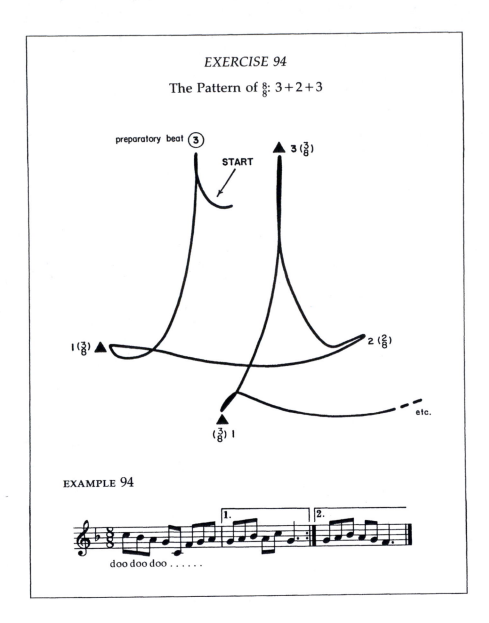

EXAMPLE 94

doo doo doo . . . . . .

Meters with Unequal Beats

EXERCISE 95

The Pattern of $\frac{8}{8}$: 3+3+2

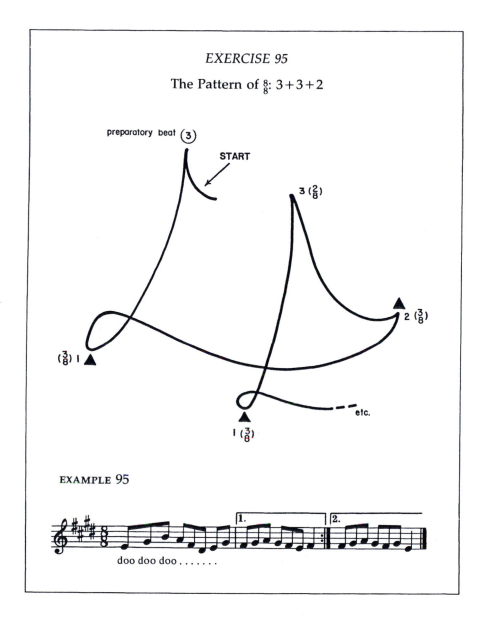

EXAMPLE 95

doo doo doo . . . .

EXERCISE 96

The Pattern of $\frac{8}{8}$ in 3, Combining Exercises 93, 94, and 95

Class members sing the example below, while students take turns conducting it with the diagrams provided in Exercises 93, 94, and 95 successively.

EXAMPLE 96

doo doo doo . . . .

Suggested Repertoire: A. Kaplan, *Sing Unto the Lord a New Song* from *Glorious*

Conducting $\frac{8}{8}$ in Four

When an $\frac{8}{8}$ measure is divided internally into four even groups of $\frac{2}{8}$, it is actually $\frac{4}{4}$ and should be conducted either in the regular or subdivided pattern of $\frac{4}{4}$, depending on the tempo. The same principle applies to all other meters of eight which are divided into four groups of two: thus, $\frac{8}{16}$ should be conducted as $\frac{4}{8}$ (or subdivision thereof); $\frac{8}{4}$ as $\frac{4}{2}$; and so on.

Conducting $\frac{9}{8}$ in Four

The meter $\frac{9}{8}$ (in a fast tempo) containing four groups of eight notes should be conducted with three short beats of $\frac{2}{8}$ each, and one longer beat of $\frac{3}{8}$. The exact sequence of long and short beats is determined by the music.

EXERCISE 97

The Pattern of $\frac{9}{8}$ in 4: $2+2+2+3$

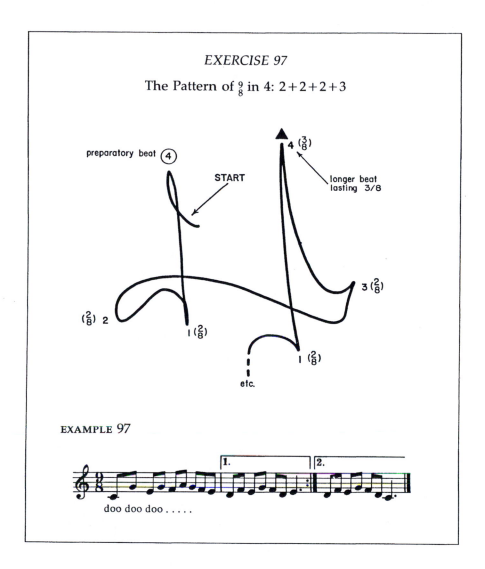

EXAMPLE 97

doo doo doo . . . . .

EXERCISE 98

The Pattern of $\frac{9}{8}$: 2+2+3+2

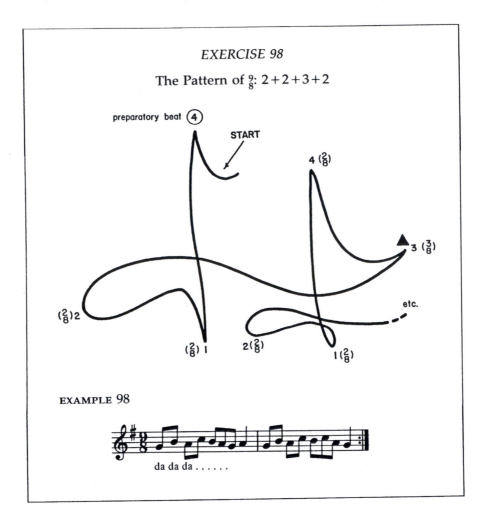

EXAMPLE 98

da da da . . . . . .

Meters with Unequal Beats

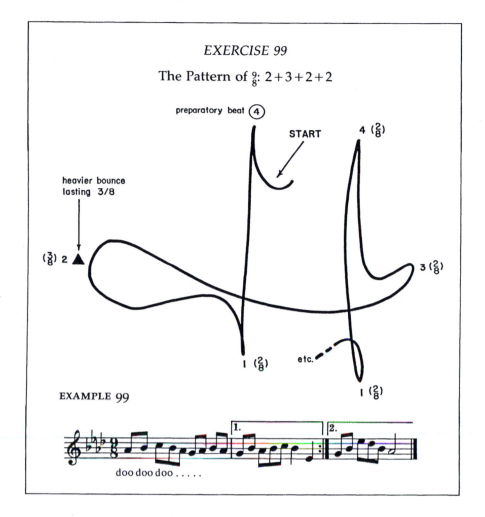

EXERCISE 99

The Pattern of $\frac{9}{8}$: 2+3+2+2

preparatory beat ④

START

4 ($\frac{2}{8}$)

heavier bounce
lasting 3/8

($\frac{3}{8}$) 2 ▲

3 ($\frac{2}{8}$)

I ($\frac{2}{8}$)

etc.

I ($\frac{2}{8}$)

EXAMPLE 99

doo doo doo . . . . .

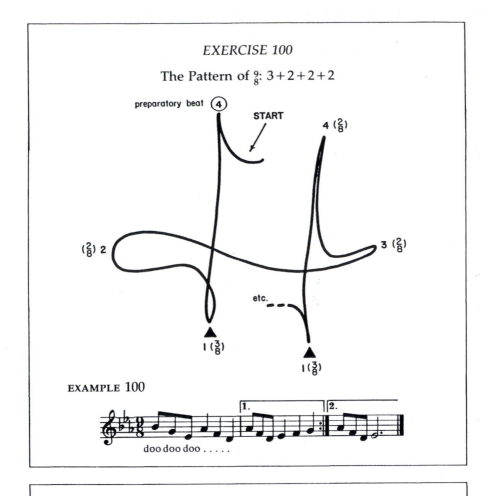

EXERCISE 100

The Pattern of $\frac{9}{8}$: 3 + 2 + 2 + 2

preparatory beat (4)

START

4 ($\frac{2}{8}$)

($\frac{2}{8}$) 2

3 ($\frac{2}{8}$)

etc.

I ($\frac{3}{8}$)

I ($\frac{3}{8}$)

EXAMPLE 100

doo doo doo . . . . .

EXERCISE 101

The Pattern of $\frac{9}{8}$ in 4, Combining Exercises 97 through 100

Class members sing the example below, while students take turns conducting it with the diagrams provided in Exercises 97 through 100 successively.

EXAMPLE 101

doo doo doo . . . . . .

Meters with Unequal Beats

Conducting $\frac{9}{8}$ in Three

When a measure of $\frac{9}{8}$ is divided internally into three groups of $\frac{3}{8}$, it is conducted in a pattern of three, or the subdivision thereof (see Chapter Eleven, *The Patterns of $\frac{12}{8}$ and $\frac{9}{8}$*).

Conducting $\frac{10}{8}$ in Four

The meter $\frac{10}{8}$ (in fast tempo) should be conducted in a pattern of four, with two long beats (of $\frac{3}{8}$ each) and two short beats (of $\frac{2}{8}$ each). The precise sequence of long and short beats is determined by the music.

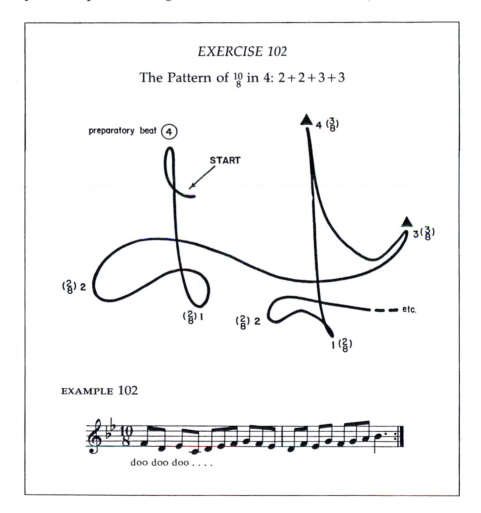

EXERCISE 102

The Pattern of $\frac{10}{8}$ in 4: 2+2+3+3

EXAMPLE 102

doo doo doo . . . .

EXERCISE 103

The Pattern of $\frac{10}{8}$: 2+3+2+3

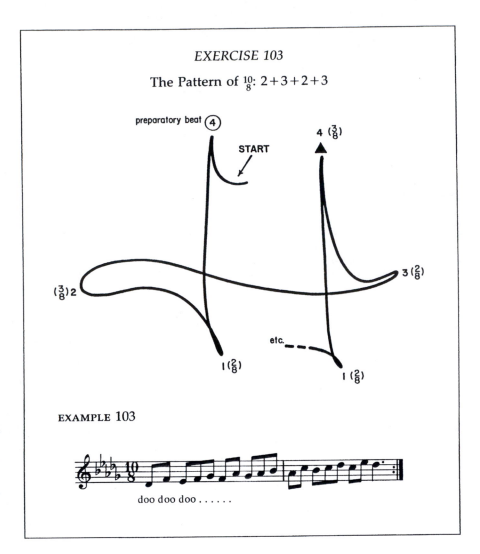

preparatory beat ④

START

4 ($\frac{3}{8}$)

($\frac{3}{8}$)2

3 ($\frac{2}{8}$)

etc.

1 ($\frac{2}{8}$)

1 ($\frac{2}{8}$)

EXAMPLE 103

doo doo doo . . . . . .

EXERCISE 104

The Pattern of $\frac{10}{8}$: 3 + 2 + 2 + 3

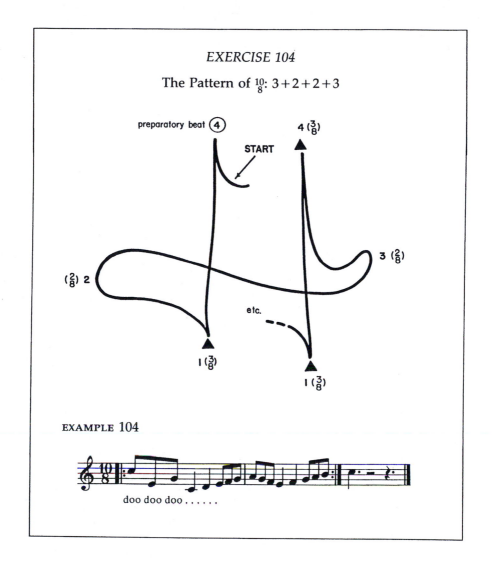

EXAMPLE 104

doo doo doo . . . . . .

EXERCISE 105

The Pattern in $\frac{10}{8}$: $3+2+3+2$

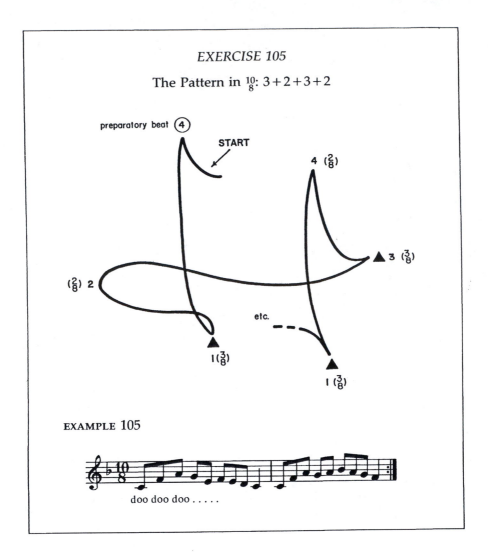

EXAMPLE 105

doo doo doo . . . . .

EXERCISE 106

The Pattern in $\frac{10}{8}$: 3+3+2+2

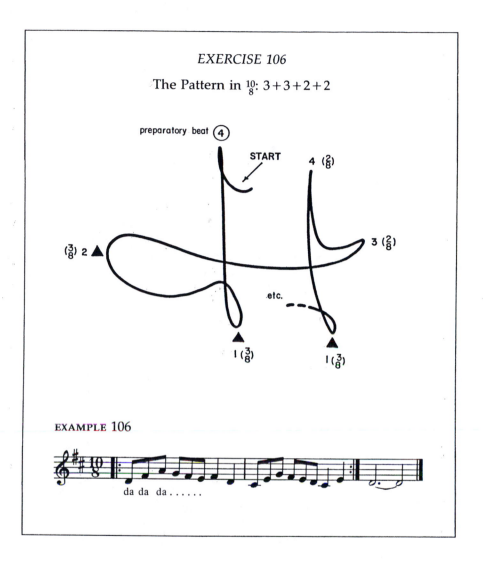

EXAMPLE 106

da da da......

EXERCISE 107

The Pattern in $\frac{10}{8}$: $2+3+3+2$

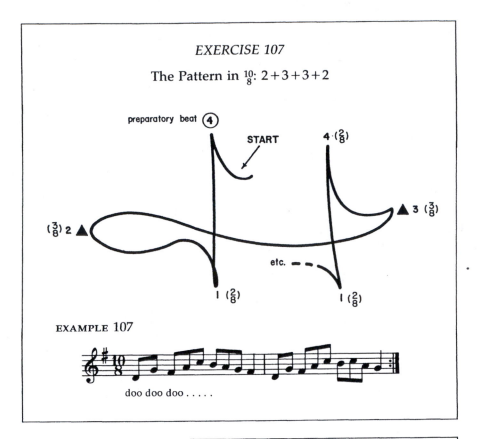

EXAMPLE 107

doo doo doo . . . . .

EXERCISE 108

The Pattern of $\frac{10}{8}$ in 4, Combining Exercises 102 through 107

Class members sing the example below, while students take turns conducting it with the diagrams provided in Exercises 102 through 107 successively.

EXAMPLE 108

da da da . . . .

Meters with Unequal Beats

Suggested Repertoire: Bernstein, *Chichester Psalms* (first movement)

Conducting $\frac{10}{8}$ in Five

When the meter $\frac{10}{8}$ is divided internally into five groups of $\frac{2}{8}$ each, it should be conducted as $\frac{5}{4}$.

Conducting $\frac{11}{8}$ in Four

When the meter $\frac{11}{8}$ is divided internally into four groups, use the pattern of four. Each measure will include three long beats of $\frac{3}{8}$ and one short beat of $\frac{2}{8}$.

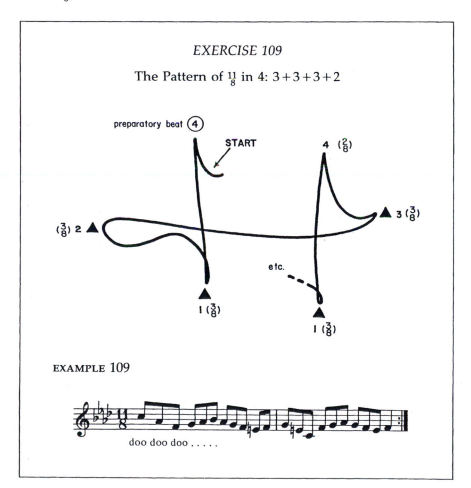

EXERCISE 109

The Pattern of $\frac{11}{8}$ in 4: $3+3+3+2$

EXAMPLE 109

doo doo doo . . . . .

EXERCISE 110

The Pattern of $\frac{11}{8}$: 3+3+2+3

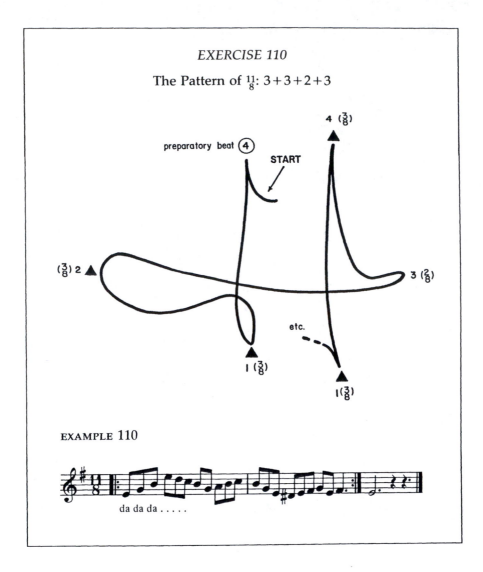

EXAMPLE 110

da da da . . . . .

EXERCISE 111

The Pattern of $\frac{11}{8}$: 3 + 2 + 3 + 3

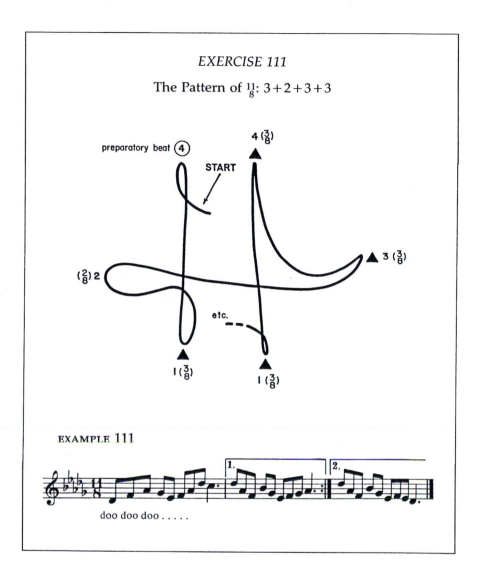

EXAMPLE 111

doo doo doo . . . . .

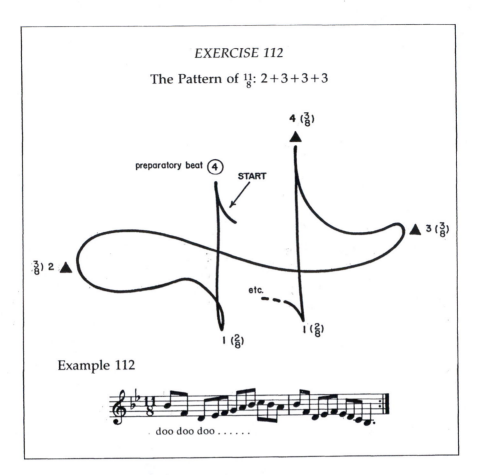

EXERCISE 112

The Pattern of $\frac{11}{8}$: 2+3+3+3

Example 112

doo doo doo . . . . . .

Conducting $\frac{11}{8}$ in Five

The most common division of the $\frac{11}{8}$ meter is into five groups, four of these consisting of $\frac{2}{8}$ and one of $\frac{3}{8}$.

EXERCISE 113

The Pattern for $\frac{11}{8}$ in 5: 2+2+2+2+3

Class members sing the example below while students take turns conducting Diagram A, then Diagram B. In both cases, the fifth beat (marked ▲) should last $\frac{3}{8}$, while all the other beats last only $\frac{2}{8}$.

Meters with Unequal Beats

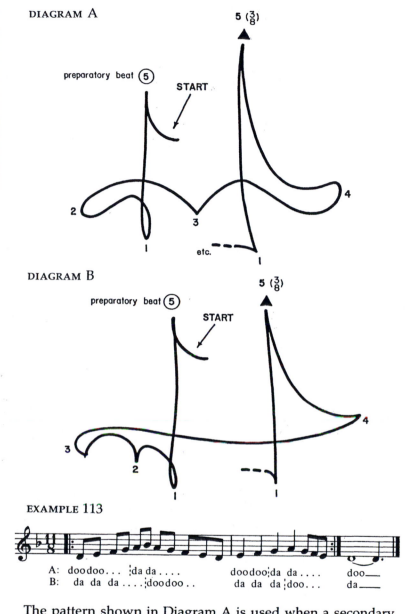

DIAGRAM A

5 ($\frac{3}{8}$)

preparatory beat (5)

START

2

3

4

1

etc.

1

DIAGRAM B

5 ($\frac{3}{8}$)

preparatory beat (5)

START

3

2

4

1

1

EXAMPLE 113

A: doo doo... ¦da da....   doo doo¦da da....   doo___
B: da da da....¦doo doo..   da da da¦doo...   da___

The pattern shown in Diagram A is used when a secondary stress is desired on the third beat of each measure. The pattern shown in Diagram B is used when the secondary stress occurs on the fourth beat of each measure. Example 113 (without accompaniment) may be conducted either way.

EXERCISE 114

The Pattern of $\frac{11}{8}$ in 5: $2+2+2+3+2$

Class members sing the example below while students take turns conducting Diagram A, then Diagram B. In both cases the fourth beat (marked ▲) should last $\frac{3}{8}$, while all the other beats last only $\frac{2}{8}$.

DIAGRAM A

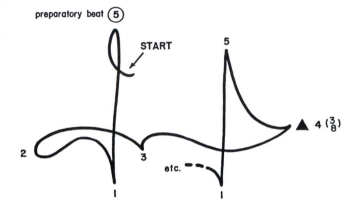

DIAGRAM B

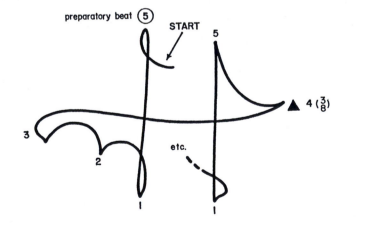

EXAMPLE 114

doo doo doo . . . . . .

Meters with Unequal Beats

EXERCISE 115

The Pattern of $\frac{11}{8}$ in 5: $2+2+3+2+2$

Class members sing the example below while students take turns conducting Diagram A, then Diagram B. In both cases, the third beat (marked ▲) should last $\frac{3}{8}$, while all other beats last only $\frac{2}{8}$.

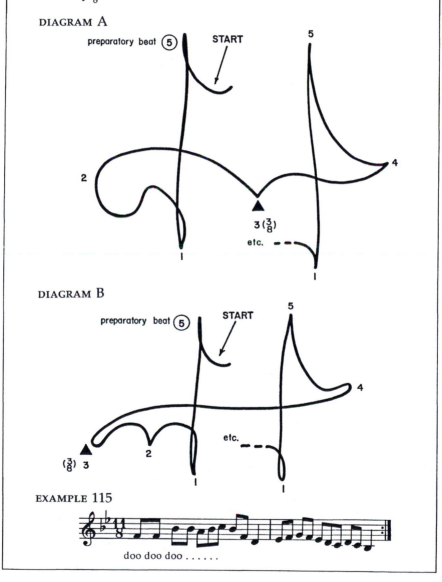

DIAGRAM A

DIAGRAM B

EXAMPLE 115

doo doo doo . . . . . .

EXERCISE 116

The pattern of $\frac{11}{8}$ in 5: $2+3+2+2+2$

Class members sing the example below while students take turns conducting Diagram A, then Diagram B. In both cases, the second beat (marked ▲)should last $\frac{3}{8}$, while all the other beats last only $\frac{2}{8}$.

DIAGRAM A

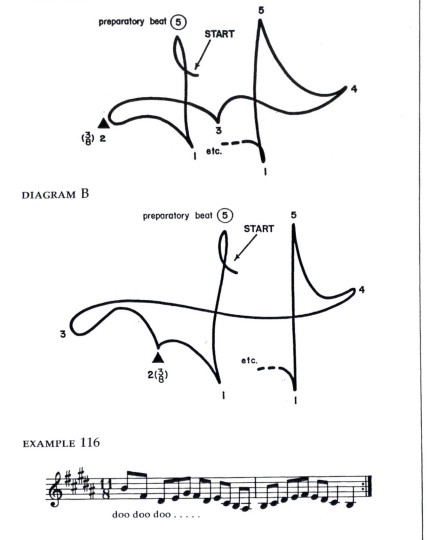

DIAGRAM B

EXAMPLE 116

doo doo doo . . . . .

EXERCISE 117

The Pattern of $\frac{11}{8}$ in 5: 3+2+2+2+2

Class members sing the example below while students take turns conducting Diagram A, then Diagram B. In both cases, the first beat (marked ▲) should last $\frac{3}{8}$, while all the other beats last only $\frac{2}{8}$.

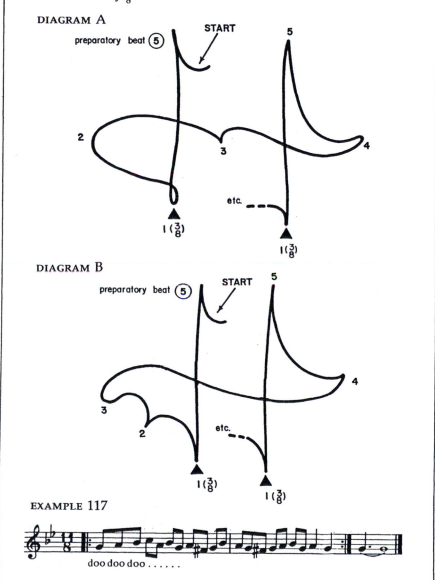

DIAGRAM A

DIAGRAM B

EXAMPLE 117

doo doo doo . . . . . .

Conducting $\frac{5}{8}$ in Two

When $\frac{5}{8}$ has to be conducted in two, each measure should include one beat lasting $\frac{3}{8}$ and one $\frac{2}{8}$, the sequence of long and short beats being determined by the inner divisions of the music.

EXERCISE 118

The Pattern of $\frac{5}{8}$ in 2: 2+3

EXAMPLE 118

doo doo doo . . . . . .

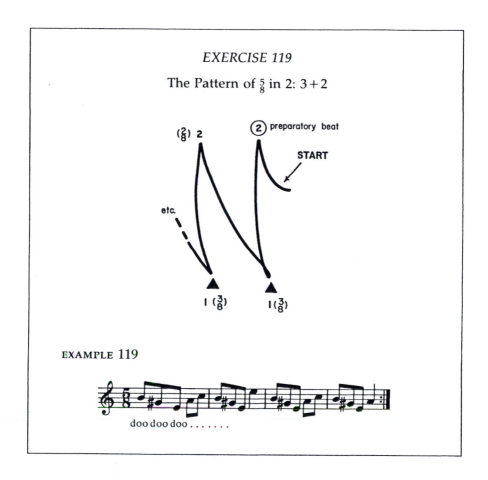

EXERCISE 119

The Pattern of $\frac{5}{8}$ in 2: 3+2

EXAMPLE 119

doo doo doo . . . .

Suggested Repertoire: Bartók, *Four Slovak Songs* (No. 2)

        A. Kaplan, *Halleluyah* from *Glorious*

        ————, "Arvit Leshabat" (*Sabbath Evening Service*)

        ————, *Who Is Like Thee*

        Bernstein, *Chichester Psalms*

        Stravinsky, *Symphony of Psalms*

        Britten, *Ceremony of Carols*

        ————, *Rejoice in the Lamb*

Chapter Fifteen

GOALS

Programming

From the first moment you start thinking about the music to be included in any program you must keep your potential audience in mind:

1. What will bring them to the concert? (Remember what the great impresario Sol Hurok once said: "If the audience chooses to stay home, nobody can stop them!")
2. Which music will be familiar and which will sound new?
3. How will that new music strike them? Will they recognize the style or will they be bewildered by it?
4. Will the overall effect of the concert be satisfying?
5. Can I, the conductor (with my limitations) and the ensemble (with its limitations) give a convincing performance of the selected repertoire?

The hardest programs to put together are those which consist of fifteen to twenty-five short choral pieces which have to be performed in some logical order. All of us have listened to a concert and thought: "The choir is superb, the music is beautiful. Why does the concert seem interminable?"

The answer is that the selections are probably being performed in the wrong sequence.

One cannot perform twenty encore-type pieces (each contrasting with its predecessor) without exhausting the audience and canceling the impact of each selection by the one that follows. It is better to have approximately four or five groups on each program, with several selections in each group.

Once the groups are chosen, they should be arranged in a sequence that allows the highest point—aesthetically and emotionally—to come at the end of the concert. This will not only result in louder and longer applause, but will also send your audience home with uplifted spirits.

Following are two examples of good programming:

PROGRAM A

Group One: Three English madrigals (breezy and light) (e.g., Morley, *Fire, Fire*)

Group Two: Three Renaissance motets (of sustained quality) (e.g., Victoria, *O vos omnes*

Group Three: Two nineteenth-century art songs for chorus with piano accompaniment (e.g., Schumann, *Zigeunerleben*)

Intermission

Group Four: Four contemporary motets (e.g., Poulenc, *Christmas Motets*)

Group Five: Three folksongs (of a rousing nature) (e.g., *Hava nagila*)

PROGRAM B

Group One: Three motets of a rousing nature (e.g., Praetorius, *En natus est Emmanuel*)

Group Two: Three motets of contemplative nature (e.g., Schein, *Die mit Tränen*)

Group Three: A cycle of folksongs (e.g., Vaughan Williams, *Five English Folksongs* or Bartók, *Four Slovak Songs*).

Intermission

Group Four: Choral art songs with piano accompaniment (e.g., Rossini, *Ave Maria*)

Group Five: Medley of choruses from musical shows

Once you have written out the complete program, give it the "audience test." Sit in your favorite chair and listen to it in your mind (or listen to actual recordings) from beginning to end.

Make changes in the order of the selections or replace them if you think it will enhance the overall effectiveness of the program.

Two more suggestions: 1) any of the groups can be replaced with a single composition of 15 to 25 minutes duration; 2) if your program consists of large compositions do not forget to give it "the audience test" to insure the right sequence.

The Ideal Rehearsal

The ideal rehearsal is one in which the most progress toward an ideal performance is achieved. Therefore the rehearsal should accomplish different things at different stages of preparation. However, most ideal rehearsals share a few very important characteristics.

If you listen to a good rehearsal, you will notice that it usually proceeds in the following manner: the chorus sings; the conductor gives a *simple, understandable* instruction; the chorus resumes singing and a change (for the better, we hope) occurs. Even if the change is not for the better and has to be modified later, the essence of a good instruction is that it is understood by the chorus and requires that they *change something* in their performance.

The ideal rehearsal also includes a certain amount of music making. An altogether technically oriented rehearsal will rarely hold the attention of even the most professional singers. And without continued attention, one cannot achieve continued productivity.

In order to give substance to these observations, I'd like to outline the planning and execution of an actual rehearsal. Let us assume that we are preparing Program A described on page 187.

Rehearsal Plan

The overall plan for this particular rehearsal would include sight reading through the first and last of Poulenc's *Christmas Motets* and continuing work already begun on Victoria's *O vos omnes*, Morley's *Fire, Fire*, and Schein's *Die mit Tränen*.

Rehearsal Sequence

1. Warm-up.
2. Schumann's *Zigeunerleben*. Start with the Schumann, because it takes most choruses between a third and half of the total rehearsal time to get really warmed up. The best pieces to rehearse during this period of continuous warm-up are those with independent piano accompaniment. The Schumann meets this criterion. (Note: If such selections are not included in the program, rehearse an *a cappella* piece with the piano doubling the parts.) In any case, during this early part of the rehearsal, try to work on compositions which have a comfortable tessitura.
3. Victoria, *O vos omnes*, with partial piano support.
4. Schein, *Die mit Tränen*.

5. Sight-read the Poulenc *Motets* with piano support.
6. Morley, *Fire, Fire*.
7. If there is any time left, run through the best-prepared selections for a maximum of musicality. The rehearsal sequence is designed to make sure the chorus warms up as gradually as possible. But it must also provide a good mixture of music making and technical work. This will guarantee the continuous attention of the singers.

Rehearsal Technique

Planning what to rehearse should be based whenever possible on what happened in the previous rehearsals. However, if you are not absolutely sure that certain problems will inevitably turn up in subsequent readings of the composition, work out a plan that addresses a specific problem, but give the chorus a chance to solve it themselves. If they do, move on to the next project.

Here is the kind of work I would do in the rehearsal described above:

Schumann: Chorus sings through the composition to confirm my impression that certain problems persist. Then, for example, I zero in on the places where a mouthful of words must be enunciated rapidly and ask the chorus to speak the text in rhythm. If they still have some difficulty, we repeat the process in a slower tempo, increasing the tempo in subsequent repeats. Then I ask the chorus to sing the same passage on a syllable like "la, la" or "doo, doo" to insure that the difficulty did not stem from an incorrect reading of the pitches. Finally, the chorus sings the passage as printed.

Victoria: In the previous rehearsal, I had difficulty getting the tenors to start the first note together. I now ask them to modify the vowel from "O" to halfway between "O" and "Oo." I don't explain; I demonstrate the sound. I also ask them to use a slight glottal attack on that first entrance. In addition, instead of conducting an accentuated downbeat, I give them an accentuated preparatory beat followed by a flowing pattern. All of this was planned ahead of time; when we start singing the composition and the tenors make their entrance successfully, they either forget that they had a problem or wonder where it went. In either case, I don't dwell on it.

Schein: I rehearse the chromatic scale by asking the singers to think of the distance between F and F♯ as two-thirds of a step (not

half); between F♯ and G as one-third of a step; between G and
G♯ as two-thirds of a step; etc.

Poulenc: We simply read through the first and last motets twice. I
mention to the chorus before starting that in *Hodie Christus natus
est,* the $\frac{6}{4}$ is conducted as a subdivided $\frac{3}{2}$.

Morley: I ask the chorus to place the final consonant "t" of "my
heart" on the following rest. I also remind myself not to conduct
the beats on which these final "t"s occur too abruptly.

On the "music-making" run through, I vary the interpretations by
changing tempos slightly and changing conducting motions. This pre-
pares the chorus to be flexible and attentive for a spontaneous performance at the concert.

The Ideal Concert

The ideal performance is one in which all participants (conductor, singers, and instrumentalists) have mastered all the technical problems and
are now ready to perform the music as if it were being improvised at
that very instant.

Epilogue

Pablo Picasso is reported to have once said, "The goal of an artist is to
draw a perfect circle. Since a perfect circle cannot be drawn, the deviations from the perfect circle will express the artist's own personality. But
if the artist tries to express his own personality by concentrating on the
deviations, he will miss the whole point."

The performing musician achieves the perfect circle by bringing to
life the works of great geniuses—the composers.

Arturo Toscanini is supposed to have remarked, "Some people see
Napoleon at the opening of Beethoven's Third Symphony, some don't.
I only see Allegro Moderato."

In the same vein, Wanda Landowska concluded a heated argu-
ment with a colleague by saying, "You perform the music of Bach *your*
way and I will perform it *his* way."

Neither of these two great artists was being flippant or arrogant.
They both spent a lifetime reaching for what they considered the "perfect circle."

The expression of our personality, which is the most important and unique contribution each of us brings to the art of music, will be manifest if we keep reaching for that "perfect circle." And though I have never achieved what I consider to be a perfect performance, I find the pursuit of this elusive goal immensely rewarding.

I hope that this book helps you in your quest for your "perfect circle." Each time you prepare for a concert, strive for the perfect performance and perhaps you will be fortunate enough to achieve it someday.

Happy Music Making!

Happy Conducting!

Appendix

SUGGESTED REPERTOIRE

The annotated list of works below includes the selections suggested in the body of the book, plus a few others which will prove helpful in perfecting the choral conductor's skills. The name of the publisher of each piece is given to facilitate purchase of the material. Where there is more than one edition currently available, I have chosen the one or two I find most useful. Those selections that appear in the Norton Historical Anthology *Choral Music* edited by Ray Robinson (New York: W. W. Norton, 1978) are indicated by the abbreviation N.H.A. Where an English translation of the title follows the original in parentheses, a singable English text is printed in the music.

Bach, Johann Sebastian (1685–1750)

Cantata No. 4: *Christ lag in Todesbanden*
Among the two hundred and eight cantatas written by J. S. Bach, *Christ lag* stands out, not only because of its beauty, but also for its remarkable form. All of the seven movements are in E minor, all are based on one chorale melody, and the overall structure is symmetrical: movements I, IV, and VII are for 4-part chorus; movements II and VI are duets; and III and V are for a solo voice. (Breitkopf & Härtel; Novello)

Chorales
The Bach chorales are probably the best musical vehicle for developing a sense of harmony and improving intonation in a chorus. They also afford almost limitless opportunities for the refinement of the conductor's technique. (G. Schirmer, *Sixteen Chorales*)

Mass in B minor
Before attempting to conduct a performance of the B-minor Mass, be sure that your conducting technique is solid. (C. F. Peters)

Jesu meine Freude (Motet No. 3, BWV 227)
This work, in eleven movements, is the composer's only chorale motet. It should be performed with some kind of accompaniment; either a continuo or with instruments doubling the vocal parts. A combination of these two is also possible. (C. F. Peters; N.H.A.)

Barber, Samuel (1910–81)

Reincarnations: Mary Hynes, Anthony O'Doyly, The Coolin'
These three compositions represent some of the best choral writing of this century. Although they are not easy to sing or conduct, they will reward your effort. (G. Schirmer; N.H.A.)

Bartók, Béla (1881–1945)

Four Slovak Songs: Wedding Song from Poniky, Song of the Hay Harvesters, Medzibrod, Dancing Song from Poniky
Charming and imaginative arrangements of folksongs. Accessible to practically every chorus. (Universal Edition; Boosey & Hawkes; N.H.A.)

Beethoven, Ludwig van (1770–1827)

Mass in C major
This deceptively easy Schubertian Mass holds many traps for the inexperienced conductor. Practice the conducting of *fp* and study the score and its surprises. Unlike other Beethoven works, this one does not pose difficulties of tessitura. (Edwin F. Kalmus (Belwin Mills); N.H.A.)

Bennet, John (fl, 1599–1614)

Let go, why do you stay me?
A fast-moving, exciting madrigal. (E. C. Schirmer)

Bernstein, Leonard (1918–91)

Chichester Psalms
One of the few choral masterpieces of the twentieth century. Though short (18½ minutes), its three movements are packed with beautiful music and profound interpretations of the psalms. The work is not too hard to sing. (Amberson Enterprises Inc.; G. Schirmer Inc. Sole Selling Agent)

Warm Up (A Round for Chorus)
This work, first published under this title, was later incorporated in the larger work *Mass* with the title "Responsory Alleluia." In its original version it was scored for *a cappella* chorus. The later version had percussion added to it. Thus the work may be performed either way. (Amberson Enterprises Inc.; G. Schimer Inc. Sole Selling Agent)

Bloch, Ernest (1880–1959)

Sacred Service: "O May the Words"
One of this century's underrated masterpieces. It is easy to sing (excellent voice leading and comfortable tessitura) and is scored brilliantly to allow an easy balance between chorus and orchestra. (Broude Bros.)

Brahms, Johannes (1833–97)

Four Folksongs: In stiller Nacht (In Shadowed Night), *Erlaubemir* (Allow Me), *Abschiedslied* (Song of Farewell), *Da untem in Tale* (Down Deep in the Valley)
Thoughtful placement of final consonants in these beautifully sustained folksongs is the first priority if one is to get the sublime performance that Brahms's compositions deserve. (Mercury Music Corp.)

Nänie
A smooth but clear conducting pattern of $\frac{6}{4}$ is absolutely essential for a good performance of this jewel-like short composition. (G. Schimer; C. F. Peters)

A German Requiem
Brahms's careful choice of texts for his *German Requiem* reveals the importance that he attributed to the text in a vocal work. One word of

caution: most of Brahms's music is performed too fast. If you are in doubt as to what the speed should be of any given movement, choose the slow one. In the *Requiem*, the fugues are a special case in point. Do not rush! (C. F. Peters)

Britten, Benjamin (1913–76)

A Ceremony of Carols
A wonderful cycle of songs for the Christmas season. Scored for treble voices and harp (or piano). Arrangement for an SATB chorus is also available. (Boosey & Hawkes)

Jubilate Deo
A short jubilant work with organ. It can be performed by most church choirs. (Oxford University Press; N.H.A.)

Dawson, William L. (1899–)

Soon Ah Will be Done (Spiritual)
A rousing, beautiful spiritual by one of the outstanding composer-arrangers of this genre. (Music Press; Tuskegee Institute, Ala.; Neil A. Kjos Music Co., Distributor)

There Is a Balm in Gilead (Spiritual)
One of the best examples of his craft for mixed voices with soprano solo. (William Dawson [Music Press]; N.H.A.)

Dvořák, Antonin (1841–1904)

In Nature: Songs Filled My Head, When Evening Comes, Chimes Fill the Forest, Golden Harvest, Up Sprang a Birch Tree, Oh, Here's a Day for Joyful Singing
The choral settings of these five folklike melodies are most appropriate for the mood that each of the texts requires. They are extremely popular with audiences and are fun to sing. (Mercury Music Corp.)

Fauré, Gabriel (1845–1924)

Cantique de Jean Racine
A gem of a work for four-voice chorus with keyboard accompaniment by this great master of color, melody, and subtle harmony. This edition includes an English text. (Broude Brothers; N.H.A.)

French Folk Dance (arr. Abraham Kaplan)

O Beautiful Young Maiden
A charming, dancelike melody arranged for chorus and tambourine. (Lawson-Gould)

German Carol (arr. Abraham Kaplan)

In dulci jubilo
One of the oldest and most beloved Christmas melodies in a new and simple arrangement. (Lawson-Gould)

Gershwin, George (1898–1937)

Song of Spring
One of the few works written by this great master for an SATB chorus and piano. It is vintage Gershwin. (Lawson-Gould; N.H.A.)

Gibbons, Orlando (1583–1625)

This Is the Record of John
An anthem with a beautifully flowing melody. Scored for SAATB with organ or piano accompaniment. (Novello; N.H.A.)

Handel, George Frideric (1685–1759)

Messiah (An Oratorio)
Since this masterwork has probably been performed more than any other composition in the history of music, it is not surprising that during the more than two hundred and forty years since it was written, many composers, editors, and other musicians have tried their hand at "improving" it. Those improvements have taken many forms, from "beefing up" the orchestration to adding dynamics to the vocal score. The latter was primarily due to a misunderstanding of Handel's method for indicating dynamic marks. For more on this subject, read my Editor's Preface in the edition mentioned here. (Charles Hansen; selling agent Capitol Music Co.)

Haydn, Franz Joseph (1732–1809)

"The Heavens are Telling" from *The Creation*
This selection is one of the most popular among church choirs. It requires solid conducting technique in order to bring off the slower tempo, the fermatas, and the return to *allegro* in a manner that does not sound belabored and feels musically natural. (C. F. Peters Corp.)

Missa in tempore belli (Mass in Time of War) *(Paukenmesse)*
A unique setting of the Mass, even when compared to the other Masses composed by Haydn. The timpani are the featured instruments not through virtuoso playing, but by depicting the atmosphere under which this work was composed (in time of war). (Edwin Kalmus; N.H.A.)

Ingalls, Jeremiah (1774–1828)

Northfield
A simple, straightforward piece in C major, somewhat reminiscent of William Billings's fuging tunes. (Edward B. Marks Music Corp.; N.H.A.)

Kaplan, Abraham (1931–)

Glorious
Glorious is a collection of 12 choral settings of biblical texts. All but one are accompanied by piano or a small instrumental ensemble. The exception is *O My Son Absalom*, which is for *a cappella* chorus. Most are written in a folk idiom. Each selection is published separately as well as in collection. A recording is also available from the publisher. The selections are as follows: *Halleluya, Praise the Lord! Amen, Have Mercy upon Me, I Will Lift up Mine Eyes unto the Hills, The Lord Is My Shepherd, My Heart Is Not Haughty, O My Son Absalom, Out of the Depths, Praise Ye, Sing unto the Lord a New Song, So God Created Man, So the Sun Stood Still, To Everything There Is a Season.* (Charles Hansen; selling agent Capitol Music Co.)

Sabbath Eve Service
This service can be performed as a concert piece with orchestral accompaniment or as a service with organ. Many of the movements can also be performed separately with accompaniment or *a cappella*. (Charles Hansen; selling agent Capitol Music Co.)

Who Is Like Thee
A short choral piece for mixed chorus and piano set in the meter of $\frac{7}{8}$. It can be performed in English, Hebrew, or a combination of both. The text is derived from the Book of Exodus. (Charles Hansen; selling agent Capitol Music Co.)

Kodály, Zoltán (1882–1967)

Missa brevis (Kyrie)
A twentieth-century choral masterpiece overlooked by most conductors. A very singable piece. (Boosey & Hawkes)

Marcello, Benedetto (1686–1739)

Maoz Tzur (Rock of Ages)
Set to the Hebrew text, it is especially appropriate for the Jewish holiday of Hanukah. (Lawson-Gould)

Mendelssohn, Felix (1809– 47)

Elijah (An Oratorio)
One of the greatest masterpieces of all times. In this piece Mendelssohn rises to heights of inspiration, craftsmanship, and profundity found only in works such as Bach's *St. Matthew Passion,* which he helped the Western world rediscover. Don't be misled by the pretty melodies that permeate this composition. Look for word painting and try to understand the dynamics. Never forget that according to Mendelssohn, God does not appear to us in the fire or the earthquake. He reveals himself to us in a "still small voice," or, as a literal translation of the original Hebrew text *b'kol dmama daka* would read, "In the voice of thin silence." (G. Schirmer)

The Lark
A wonderful, fun piece written by a great craftsman. If the tessitura is too high for the chorus, do not hesitate to transpose this composition to a lower key. (Music 70)

Mennin, Peter (1923 – 83)

On the Han River
An excellent piece for practice in conducting in 5. (Carl Fischer)

Morley, Thomas (1557–1603)

Fire, Fire
A rousing ballett, quite tricky rhythmically, with a "fa la la" refrain. Definitely an audience favorite. Scored for SSATB. (G. Schirmer; N.H.A.)

Mozart, Wolfgang Amadeus (1756–91)

Ave Verum Corpus
In Mozart compositions, *adagio* coupled with a ₵ *(alla breve)* time signature should be conducted in 4 most of the time. Thus if you conduct *Ave Verum Corpus* as ♩=80–96, the half note will be M.M. 40–56, which is an appropriate range for adagio. (Breitkopf & Hartel; N.H.A.)

Coronation Mass (K. 317)
A good piece for a conductor and chorus who are going to sing with orchestra for the first time. The Kyrie should be conducted in 8 (subdivided 4). When the change of tempo occurs, conducting should change to 4, with the quarter note equaling the preceding eighth note. Since transition occurs in the middle of the measure, the pattern of the transition measure should appear as follows: one and two and three four. (Breitkopf & Härtel; N.H.A.)

Poulenc, Francis (1899–1963)

Four Christmas Motets: O Magnum Mysterium, Quem Vidistis Pastore, Videntes Stellam, Hodie Christus.
These beautiful, simple-sounding compositions need a first-rate conductor and chorus to perform them successfully. (Salabert)

Praetorius, Michael (1571–1621)

En natus est Emmanuel (Born is the Lord Emmanuel)
A light, happy Christmas anthem. (E. C. Schirmer)

Purcell, Henry (1659–95)

Come, Ye Sons of Art
This wonderful, sunny cantata, written to celebrate the birthday of Queen Mary, wife of William III, can be performed, if necessary, with piano.

The first movement is best known today. (Schott & Co.; N.H.A. [lst movement])

Rossini, Gioacchino (1792–1868)

Ave Maria (Hail Mary)
A novelty from this great opera composer. (Lawson-Gould)

Saint Saëns, Camille (1835–1921)

Ave Verum Corpus
A simple and touching short motet. (Lawson-Gould)

Schubert, Franz (1808–78)

Mass No. 2 in G
The great popularity of the work with amateur choruses is well deserved. The pretty melodies are set in a manner that suggests maturity of composition technique, an amazing fact when you consider that Schubert wrote this Mass at the age of seventeen or eighteen. (Broude Brothers)

Schumann, Robert (1810–56)

Zigeunerleben (A Gypsy's Life)
A short, amusing piece for SATB with a piano accompaniment which reflects the text, highlighting the important moments. (Lawson-Gould; N.H.A.)

Schütz, Heinrich (1585–1672)

Der Psalm 98 (Sing unto the Lord)
One of the outstanding examples of double chorus writing. Scored for two SATB choirs, it can be performed *a cappella*, with brass ensemble (4 trumpets and 4 trombones) or other accompaniment. For full effect place the two choruses as far from each other as possible. Do not hesitate to transpose the work to the key that will result in the best tessitura for your chorus. (Belwin Mills)

Stravinsky, Igor (1882–1971)

Ave Maria
A short and beautiful *a cappella* motet. It can be performed by any chorus that is capable of singing music in four parts. (Boosey & Hawkes)

Mass
Scored for mixed chorus and 10 instruments, this work is a wonderful chamber piece. There are no big climaxes, but a succession of beautiful, uniquely Stravinskian sounds. It is somewhat reminiscent of the Greek Orthodox liturgy. (Boosey & Hawkes; N.H.A.)

Symphony of Psalms
One of Stravinsky's greatest compositions, it is scored for chorus and orchestra. However, the scoring is not for the usual symphony orchestra. It does not, for example, require any violins. Thus, study the orchestration before you include this work in your program. (Boosey & Hawkes)

Tallis, Thomas (1505–83)

If Ye Love Me
One of the most beloved motets of all times. (Novello)

Vaughan Williams, Ralph (1872–1958)

Five English Folksongs
These songs can be performed as a cycle, individually or in groups of three. (Galaxy Music Corp.)

Verdi, Giuseppe (1813–1901)

Quattro pezzi sacri: Ave Maria
An amazing and unique creation from this great composer. This is one of the hardest compositions to perform well. It is scored for *a cappella* chorus. It is very chromatic, with enharmonic changes of the Bruckner variety, and it is based on what Verdi called an "Enigmatic Scale," which is hard to sing in tune. However, the hard work it requires yields great rewards. (Edward B. Marks Music Corp.; N.H.A).

Requiem (First Movement)
This work should be undertaken only after the conductor has had vast experience conducting both chorus and orchestra. (C. F. Peters)

Victoria, Thomas Luis de (1548–1611)

Ave Maria, O magnum mysterium, and *O vos omnes*
Pier Luigi da Palestrina, in an introduction to a volume of motets written by his twenty-two-year-old student Victoria, acknowledges that he has learned a new expressive style from his young student, thereby reaffirming the old adage that it takes genius to recognize genius. The wonderful, expressive quality of Victoria's motets has not diminished with the passage of time. (*Ave Maria*—G. Schirmer; *O magnum mysterium, O vos omnes*—E. C. Schirmer)

Vivaldi, Antonio (1678–1741)

Gloria
If you have not conducted a chorus with orchestra yet, this piece is one of the best compositions with which to start. (Walton Music Corp.)

Walton, Sir William Turner (1902–83)

Belshazzar's Feast
Only a conductor very experienced with chorus and orchestra should undertake this work. (Oxford University Press)

Weber, Carl Maria von (1786–1826)

Mass in G
This piece, with its exuberance and dance-like melodies, exudes a charm similar to that of Schubert's *Mass in G*. It has been temporarily forgotten, but will inevitably attain the popularity it deserves. (Lawson-Gould)

Index